THE EUROPEAN PARLIAMENT, MASS MEDIA AND THE SEARCH FOR POWER AND INFLUENCE

The European Parliament, Mass Media and the Search for Power and Influence

DAVID MORGAN
Emeritus Professor, University of Liverpool;
Hon. Research Fellow, School of European Studies, Cardiff University

LONDON AND NEW YORK

First published 1999 by Ashgate Publishing

Reissued 2018 by Routledge
2 Park Square, Milton Park, Abingdon, Oxon, OX14 4RN
52 Vanderbilt Avenue, New York, NY 10017

Routledge is an imprint of the Taylor & Francis Group, an informa business

Copyright © David Morgan 1999

All rights reserved. No part of this book may be reprinted or reproduced or utilised in any form or by any electronic, mechanical, or other means, now known or hereafter invented, including photocopying and recording, or in any information storage or retrieval system, without permission in writing from the publishers.

Notice:
Product or corporate names may be trademarks or registered trademarks, and are used only for identification and explanation without intent to infringe.

Publisher's Note
The publisher has gone to great lengths to ensure the quality of this reprint but points out that some imperfections in the original copies may be apparent.

Disclaimer
The publisher has made every effort to trace copyright holders and welcomes correspondence from those they have been unable to contact.

A Library of Congress record exists under LC control number: 99071889

ISBN 13: 978-1-138-35251-3 (hbk)
ISBN 13: 978-1-138-35253-7 (pbk)
ISBN 13: 978-0-429-43472-3 (ebk)

Contents

List of Tables vi
Acknowledgements viii

1 The European Parliament – a Parliament-in-Waiting 1

2 The European Parliament – Situation and Powers 8

3 The European Parliament, Members, Issues 14

4 British News Coverage of the European Union 24

5 British Newspapers and EU News 39

6 MEPs, Constituencies, Parties, Mass Media 48

7 MEPs and Media Coverage – the Belgian and Irish Cases
   *with John Fitzmaurice (European Commissioner) and Professor
   A.C. Collins (University College Cork, Republic of Ireland)* 69

8 Conclusions and Epilogue 92

References 100

List of Tables

Table 4.1	Press coverage of EU issue areas in 15 member states, February–November 1996 %	25
Table 4.2	Press coverage of European Union institutions, February–November 1996 %	27
Table 4.3	Monthly averages for television coverage, February–November 1996 %	28
Table 4.4	Television coverage – UK and 5 EU countries, February–November 1996 %	29
Table 4.5	BBC 9p.m. and ITN 10p.m. news coverage, May–November 1996	31
Table 4.6	Average number of pages per newspaper, minus advertisements – selected newspapers	32
Table 4.7	Average daily number of news items, February–November 1996 – selected newspapers	33
Table 4.8a	News items, European Union, May–July 1996 %	35
Table 4.8b	European Parliament, May–July 1996 %	35
Table 4.9a	News items, European Union, September–November 1996 %	37
Table 4.9b	European Parliament, September–November 1996 %	37
Table 7.1	Euromedia – selected issue area coverage – EU, UK, Belgium, July and November 1996	70
Table 7.2	Newsholes – *La Libre Belgique* and *Le Soir*, July 1996	71
Table 7.3	EU/EP news – *La Libre Belgique* and *Le Soir*, July 1996	71
Table 7.4	European Parliament news – *La Libre Belgique* and *Le Soir*, weekly average	71
Table 7.5	Euromedia – selected issue area coverage – EU, UK and Ireland, July and November 1996	82
Table 7.6	Newsholes – Irish national newspapers, May–July 1996	82
Table 7.7	EU/EP news – Irish national newspapers, May–July 1996	82
Table 7.8	European Parliament news – Irish national newspapers, May–July 1996	83

Table 7.9	EU/MEP news – Irish provincial press, May–July 1996	84
Table 7.10	European Parliament news – Irish national newspapers, May–July 1996	84
Table 7.11	Irish Television (RTE) – EP coverage, May–July 1996	85

Acknowledgements

I am grateful to the European Commission (D G X) which provided a grant allowing me to extend my research into the European Parliament. In particular I thank Madame Anna Melich and her staff in the Public Opinion Analysis Unit at D G X who, by telephone and fax, provided invaluable guidance on several matters.

The research could never have been done without the willingness of 43 MEPs and some of their staffs to give me of their time and views. All, I hope, will see that I have protected their anonymity. I wish to record my gratitude to many busy people, some of whom had learned to be very dubious about research and researchers. I am compelled to break the rule of anonymity in two particular cases. Without the encouragement and assistance of Mike Tappin, MEP and Cheryllyn Humphreys, his research assistant, the work would neither have been begun nor completed. Both had to endure an infrequent, but occasionally demanding, visiting friend while conducting their normal round of business.

I thank John Fitzmaurice who contributed the section on Belgium and Professor A.C. Collins who did likewise for the section on the Irish Republic – their assistance gave the work a needed comparative dimension.

For hospitality I owe debts to many friends but most of all to John Wyles and Carla Cimenetti who always made Brussels visits memorable.

I thank my Liverpool research assistant, Katy Parry, for her cheerfulness and industry. Errors of omission and commission in the research and writing must, of course, lie at my door.

David Morgan
Emeritus Professor
University of Liverpool;
Hon. Research Fellow
School of European Studies
Cardiff University

1 The European Parliament – a Parliament-in-Waiting

... we must now talk of the European Parliament as a major player ... (Elmar Brok MEP, 1997).

Greater powers for the European Parliament make the European Union a more democratic place (Brendan Donnelly MEP, 1997).

The Democratic Deficit

The processes of European integration have never been easy. The European Economic Community (EEC) and the European Community (EC) have well documented 'low periods', in the 1960s and 1980s, during which the future direction of integration, if not the process itself, was in doubt (George, 1990; Nugent, 1989). Given the scope of the undertaking such events need cause no surprise. By the late 1990s, however, the stakes have been raised considerably as the European Union (EU) simultaneously faces monetary union under a central European bank and tries to establish a common foreign and defence policy at a time of both high unemployment and the admission of economically weak Central European states. Additionally there are considerable Union tensions over immigration, trade problems with the USA, and the possibility of defecting member states (Duignan and Gann, 1994).

It is hardly surprising in such a context that calls for democratic accountability and transparency revived. In March 1993 what became known as the De Clercq Report – *Reflection on Information and Communication Policy of the European Community* – was finalised. It argued that 'There is no strategic direction for Community communication', (p. 4) and, inter alia, referred to the European Parliament as 'the guarantor of pluralism and democracy' (p. 15). It called for the creation of an Office of Communication under a Commissioner who would have direct access to the President (p. 43). The Office, 'in so far as communication activities are concerned' should, the Report proposed, be responsible for all Directorates General and Commission offices in member states (p. 43). The Commissioner should harmonise all Community communications, target special publics (women, youth, journalists, etc.) and ensure much greater use and reliance on audio-visual communication (De Clercq, 1993, p. 17). Given the fundamental implications of its proposals it is unsurprising that the Report was greeted with caution and not implemented.

Arguably the European Parliament (EP) has been the principal victim of the failure to implement the Report's proposals. In 1995 a partisan study of the EU characterised Parliament, despite Maastricht, as 'the Union's weakest institution' and blamed the French and British governments for that situation (Tartwyk-Novey, p. 96). In January 1996 the Hill and Knowlton Report on Parliament's communication policy concluded 'There is no structured communication policy of the European Parliament' (Hill and Knowlton, p. 63) and suggested several steps to improve the situation. Addressing the position of Parliament within EU generally, Juliet Lodge anatomised the confusions and the difficulties present in most debates on both subjects. She noted:

> Unless the European Parliament uses opportunities to highlight publicly (or to embarrass) governments over spending plans or failures ... its activities remain invisible to the public eye ... Overall, the unintentional effect of Euro-elections perhaps has been indirectly to heighten scepticism about the EU's democratic legitimacy, effectiveness and the appropriateness of its institutional arrangements (Lodge et al., 1996, pp. 212–13).

During 1996 two scholars examined the goals of European integration and pointed to their ambiguities. John Crawley noted that 'integration' as used could mean either a long term socio-economic process (convergence), a political construction, or a symbolic process (European identity) or finally '... prudential cooperation between states and non-state bodies ...' (Crawley, 1996, p. 150). Following this Philip Schlesinger, while acknowledging the importance of cultural and industrial defence, called for 'the building of a new political culture' which could manage 'the persistence of national difference' (Schlesinger, 1996, p. 24). In November 1996, prior to the Dublin Summit, the EU launched a Citizens First programme aimed at persuading European voters, as the Parliament President put it, that EU is 'a lot more than simply the commercial marketplace or a faceless, cold bureaucracy', and asserted that the Parliament had a key role in changing such perceptions (*EP News (Irish)*, 9–13 December, 1996, p. 2). A week earlier *The European* had published the results of a Mori poll in the UK showing declining general support for EU membership except, interestingly, among the young and the affluent who wanted continued membership by margins, respectively, of 20 per cent and 28 per cent (*The European*, 5–11 December 1996, p. 10).

By early 1997 the same newspaper was carrying a long interview with the new Parliament President, Jose Maria Gil-Robles. In it he advocated uniform election procedures among members for the 1999 elections, intergovernmental 'flexibility' on integration except on 'single market and competition law' but refused to contemplate any veto of integration measures by a single country. As for the Parliament, the President wanted MEPs to spend more time publicising Parliament in their constituencies but warned that member governments held the key to more powers. 'Parliament itself must prove that it can exert the power it has already and can do so properly' he added (*The European*, 23–29 January 1997, p. 9). Two weeks later, Commission President Jacques Santer asserted that he opposed an 'à la carte Europe which was,' he said, 'an unacceptable dilution'. He denied, however, that he wanted a European super state, 'If we are creating a federal state,' he said, 'it's a federal state of nations' (*The European*, 13–19 February 1997, p. 8).

Such concerns over the goal of integration are rooted in two developments. These are, firstly, the momentum acquired by the Commission, the Court and the Council of Ministers and, secondly, the relative weakness of the Parliament in relation both to Union institutions and member governments (Tartwyk-Novey 1995). Parliament has long voiced demands for greater accountability (Petersen, 1997). The 'democratic deficit' was reduced by the Maastricht Treaty and has been further reduced by the recent Amsterdam Summit. There the Parliament acquired an equal say in 23 new legislative fields – including transport, anti-fraud policies, public health, control over the financing of any foreign policy and a virtual veto over the appointment of Commission Presidents. Parliament, for the first time, was also authorised to draft proposals for a common electoral system for member states.

Elmar Brok, a Christian Democrat MEP, who represented the Parliament at the Summit, said 'we must now talk of the European Parliament as a major player ... Amsterdam has given it more power than the Maastricht Treaty did'. Klaus Haensch, the former Parliament President, added that the extra powers allowed Parliament to offset qualified majority voting in the Council of Ministers which took away some of the power of national parliaments. For him 'It only makes sense to give the European Parliament a say, to maintain democratic balance' (*The European*, 26 June –2 July 1997, p. 7). Brendan Donnelly, a Conservative MEP and no Europhile, had a letter in *The Times* a few days later. He rejected Home Secretary Michael Howard's anger at the loss of Westminster influence saying

> Greater powers for the European Parliament make the European Union a more democratic place. If that extra power is at the expense of national ministers and national civil servants, who are currently subject to only limited Parliamentary scrutiny, so be it (*The Times*, 7 July 1997).

Amsterdam was a watershed for the Parliament and convinced many members that they must close the gap between popular perceptions of Parliamentary weakness and irrelevance and the facts of growing Parliamentary power and influence. For such members an educational campaign must be begun among European voters to correct this misperception. Such members see that this means a sustained campaign at all levels and particularly a campaign to mobilise the mass media.

Parliament and Public Communication

The outlook for a change in mass media coverage, however, is mixed. Market pressures, deregulation and technical change have eroded established patterns of media coverage and consumption to the extent that national governments find more difficulty determining their popular political agendas. The ethic of public service broadcasting has weakened in face of a growing number of terrestrial and satellite channels and transnational news services. Hence efforts by European institutions including Parliament to publicise their aims and activities – to go around national governments' agenda-setting – stand a better chance of access and effectiveness than hitherto. The other side of the coin, however, is the fact that globalised media trends do not favour the cause of European integration and, particularly, are hostile to EU regulation (Dyson and Humphreys, 1986).

The literature on political communication is considerable and rapidly growing. Within that literature the roles and impact of mass media coverage have long been a central concern (Curran and Seaton, 1988; McQuail, 1992). Decades ago, Bernard Cohen noted that media 'do not tell you what to think, but are strikingly successful at telling you what to think about' (Cohen, 1963). Later studies in the 1970s and 1980s have suggested that democratic governments can often be successful at telling media 'what to think about' (Morgan, 1986, 1991). That situation is changing and presents opportunities for the EU and its proselytising.

The rise of television to a dominant position within media led to studies of its interaction with other media and its intrinsic qualities as a medium of effective mass communication. It seems clear that media coverage can be very significant in setting the political agenda for voters and that competition between media – so-called broadcast ratings and newspaper 'wars' – creates a dynamic which political elites often find damaging both to their public and private lives. The hourly interactions between television, radio and newspaper agendas in almost all countries has been intensified by rapid technical change so that, in news terms at least, the 'global village' seems no longer a fanciful notion.

Mass media effects are so obvious and potent that political leaderships have little choice but to try to set the agenda for media whenever they can. This involves proactive measures to limit the impact of bad news when governments can anticipate it, and, even more, when they cannot do so. In many countries, journalists assert, governments store good news – 'weddings' – to release when bad news – 'funerals' – hit them. Political institutions, in short, cannot afford passivity – they must seem to be transparent and active (Harris, 1990).

What is the ground of media influence? Quite simply it is the purveying of persuasive information to citizens in pictures, sound and print. Dramatic pictures, especially, have great impact when they appear in a context voters can relate to. Television gives audiences a sense of immediacy and engagement which no other medium can match. Television news coverage gives issues a higher salience in people's minds and primes them for more news to come. It also frames information in ways that can be crucial to audience response. The episodic quality of much television news, and the absence of contextual information, makes television more an illustrative than an explanatory medium. Television news formats are held to foster short-term audience engagement and understanding and, in the USA, are held responsible for audiences which appear to be the least informed among those in developed countries. Further, the impact of television is greatest among the least educated voters – those who rarely pay attention to news can sometimes be most affected by it. Overall mass audiences, including the least educated, can nevertheless absorb more information from television news if it seeks to inform and not primarily to entertain. As one study of American television noted 'the differences between NBC and the BBC matter' (Dimmock and Popkin, 1997, p. 223).

The print press, still widely read in developed countries, does not offset this information deficit. As newspapers struggle to survive as news suppliers, they are tending to provide less 'hard news' and more 'soft' interpretive material which can have the effect of altering the impact of the information they purvey, sometimes greatly. Further, newspapers have to massage the political loyalties of their readerships, and gain new readers, and this again can lead to a misrepresentation of significant political news.

EU news has to exist in this context. News of integration in all aspects has to compete with a host of alternative news stories, political and otherwise. All stories, so far as national audiences are concerned, are filtered through national media systems which are routinely influenced by national leaderships and party, personal and ideological attachments which are not always publicly clarified. In EU states the Council of Ministers and the Commission have been seen as the focus of decision making. Given the secrecy surrounding Council deliberations this has usually meant that the Commission has borne the brunt of popular discontent. Until recently the Parliament has not received much attention and hence, as will be seen, has a much lower salience among European audiences. We will need to examine what kind of news the EU makes and who makes it. If information levels are crucial to the mobilisation of electorates, then the amount and kind of information supplied about EU is a crucial matter. Given European parliamentary traditions this may be especially true for the EP in the 1990s.

While the need for better Parliamentary communication is true in all member states it is nowhere more true than in the UK. This study will examine the nature of the difficulties in the UK, Belgium and Ireland. Before those national situations are examined it will be necessary to set Parliament in its EU context – institutional, historical and political. Equally it is necessary to clarify the assumptions behind this research. We assume that the success of European integration – either into a federal union or a confederate union of states – will ultimately depend on popular acceptance and that this will be expressed via national governments and in the European Parliament. It follows that every effort must be made by EU institutions to inform and mobilise popular support by every means possible and, perhaps especially, through mass media. Implicit in this, of course, is the acceptance of the proposition that 'integration by stealth' – a tactic of the past – has become unacceptable. In this context it is assumed the member governments and national media will not be used to frustrate the necessary level of communication.

In political science terms the approach adopted will be that of the 'new institutionalism' which qualifies both 'behaviourist 'reliance on social contexts and economic forces and 'rational choice' reliance on the optimising behaviour of individual and group agents. While accepting that both approaches can make crucial contributions, the 'new institutionalism' emphasises the importance of the state and the patterns of interaction between its institutions (Skocpol, 1985). Thus we must be concerned with the real significance of the evolving formal and informal institutional relationships within the EU. Equally we must be concerned with examining the constraints on the information flow to European voters without which popular mobilisation in support of European integration will be impossible. We assume that the pattern of information flows reflects elite perceptions of the distribution of power within EU. Such perceptions frame the Parliament and make it difficult to change perceptions in line with changes in Parliament's actual power and influence. Institutions which possess acknowledged power – member governments, the Commission and the Council of Ministers – are usually reluctant to share their power and may for some time resist sharing by dominating the news agenda. We will see that such institutions tell journalists 'not what to think, but what to think about' and this capability is of considerable consequence for the Parliament in its search for power, influence and democratic accountability.

2 The European Parliament – Situation and Powers

> The European Parliament will have to have more power before it acquires more visibility (EP official, 1996).

> MEPs have no real status unless they bring it with them here. It bothers them greatly that this is the case (aide to MEP, 1996).

The Parliament and its Situation

The European Parliament seeks more power and influence and, unless the EU accepts its 'democratic deficit' as inevitable, it may have to be given both. Quite why the Parliament lacks real power and influence is a complex question which has well-rehearsed constitutional and political explanations. These are mostly reducible to the unwillingness of member governments to yield the required security, fiscal and economic powers to the Parliament. In consequence, it is said, the vehicles for these governments – the Council of Ministers and the Commission – will overtly or covertly ensure that Parliament acquires new powers slowly, if at all (Lodge, 1996).

The rationale for such behaviour is put in democratic terms. Only national parliaments, it is argued, command popular assent; Parliament is at best a genuine EU Parliament in-the-making and, at worst, an expensive 'talking shop' which is irrelevant to overseeing the EU's still modest bureaucracy. For those who see EU as a union of states, Parliament cannot be the vehicle for the articulation of popular will since this is expressed by national parliaments and, in the Council, through the governments they sustain. For those who see the EU as a union of peoples, Parliament is more significant but, until the grip of national governments is relaxed, Parliament has to be considered as a parliament-in-waiting. For the moment, and for both groups, Parliament has to be seen as an institution in transition. Crucial for this transition is increased visibility which is seen by MEPs as necessary for increasing political legitimacy without which, they think, there is no prospect of increased power and influence. Parliament's transitional status is, perhaps, reflected in the size of its Secretariat. This increased from 1,995 posts in 1979 to more than 3,500 by 1995 (Corbett et al., 1995, pp. 179–85).

The views of MEPs may be self-interested but, in fact, are well supported by research on the processes of public communication. Studies of the effects of both face-to-face and mass communication attest to the persuasiveness not of overt propaganda but of information from sources trusted by audiences. Trustworthiness is crucial since the failure to establish it triggers audience defence mechanisms which in turn downgrade the information and weaken its persuasiveness. Audiences, in short, are persuaded by information they regard as new and trustworthy – and the process is at least as much unconscious as conscious. Political 'trust' is thus only earned by institutions with a record of visible, competent public service and utility (Iyengar and Kinder, 1987).

Parliament's problems in achieving such trust are considerable. Parliament is new not old, relatively powerless not powerful, relatively invisible not prominent and by its very nature has difficulty advancing the esteem in which it is held. The 'newness' is obvious since Parliament has been directly elected for less than 20 years and it is, after all, the Parliament of a would-be federation which itself is only twice that age. By contrast most national parliaments – sometimes on shaky historic evidence – believe that they are at least a century old, while some member states claim at least five times that longevity. Parliament is, additionally, less powerful because the Commission is not a government but, in part, the instrument of member governments whose authority ultimately rests on national parliamentary institutions.

Novelty, relative powerlessness and competing parliaments are, however, not Parliament's only problems. Additionally, there are problems stemming from the fact that it is set within a federation whose powers are still uncertain and whose procedures are often slow, arcane and sometimes at variance with its rhetoric. The evolution of the US Congress serves as a useful comparison. For nearly 150 years the federal government and Congress were only intermittently powerful, the states and localities being more significant for the voters of a polity which had been intentionally fractionated by its founders. The Civil War apart, not until the twentieth century, with its frequent economic and military crises, did the federal government and Congress achieve the level of dominance they currently exercise. As Adlai Stevenson noted decades ago, the US was more 'a uniting states' than a United States down to the 1940s – its nationalism being qualified by sectional and ethnic loyalties. It must be added, however, that when tested by the internal crises of the Civil War or the Great Depression, or by external crises after 1914, American nationalism embodied in a presidentially-led federal government passed the test and seized the centre of the political stage (Greenstein, 1980).

Parliament thus might console itself over long-term possibilities – hopefully at lesser prices. In the short term, however, its complex procedures, split site location and the fact that it shares powers with the Commission and Council do not justify optimism. As will be seen, some British journalists make much of these points. MEPs, they think, are worthy of little notice since they are, as one put it, 'members of a house of those who hope for a shelf life and those who have passed their sell-by date'. For politicians, especially party leaders, national reputations and power are still the real prizes to gain. In the European Union the Parliament still appears to be something of an 'also ran'.

Mention was made earlier of the procedures of Parliament. Once again the US Congress and its history is instructive. Its media coverage focuses more on the drama of hearings with their rivalries, scandals, and conflicts with presidents, than on the details of the legislative and policy process. Journalists in Washington complain about arcane procedures and are inclined to treat them either as cover for indefensible behaviours or ignore them totally (Davidson and Oleszek, 1990). Thus Congress is too often presented either as an impotent talking shop or an unfortunate obstacle to rational White House policy making – both presentations being travesties of the truth (Paletz and Entman, 1981). Much of the same is said of the European Parliament, equally to its discredit. Even the British Parliament, especially the Commons, is often similarly presented despite the tailoring of its style and procedures to media needs. Question time, for example, with its structured political theatre, makes excellent television and used to be thought educative for voters. It is now tending to be seen by journalists and academics as mere theatre and devoid of real policy significance (Norton, 1995). Legislatures in a variety of systems, it appears, have difficulty establishing their credibility in the eyes of central bureaucracies, mass media and voters.

Parliament and its Powers

The European Parliament has been the junior partner among European institutions – overshadowed and on occasion ignored by the more powerful

Commission, Council of Ministers and on occasion Court of Justice. Parliament began life as the European Assembly of the original Coal and Steel Community not calling itself a Parliament until 1962 and not being directly elected until 1979.

Parliament's avenues of influence are currently threefold. On legislation, although the Commission under the Treaty has a monopoly of the right to table draft community legislation (right of initiative), Parliament can press the Commission to use this right in the way Parliament desires, notably via the mechanism of the 'own initiative report'. Once legislation has been put forward by the Commission, Parliament deliberates on it before the Council does so. Until recently, this was largely a matter of Parliament simply being consulted and giving its opinion, with the decision remaining entirely in the hands of the Council. In 1987 the Single European Act strengthened Parliament's position by providing for a second reading, but with the final say still in the hands of Council if it is unanimous. Since Maastricht, a co-decision procedure giving Parliament an equal say with the Council in the adoption of legislation has been crucial in giving Parliament a 'bottom line' power comparable to that of national parliaments i.e. legislation requires its approval to come into force. Under Maastricht this only applies to some areas, but will be extended by the Amsterdam Treaty to most non-agricultural legislation. Finally, Parliament has shared budgetary powers with the Council since 1975 – a fact which gives it potential for real leverage in this area. As one MEP observed 'we can pass the laws we want and stop the laws we don't want'.

The weaknesses of Parliament are a corollary of its strengths. Once Parliament gives an Opinion it has to accept that the Council of Ministers, if unanimous, can still overturn amendments which have been accepted by the Commission. However, both the Council and Commission now report back to Parliament and the Single European Act, by establishing a second Reading for bills, makes these Reports more meaningful. The Commission and Council can play on any weaknesses, however. One is that the Council may feel driven by circumstances to decide an issue before Parliament gives an Opinion. Others are that the Commission and not Parliament is responsible for regulations created in pursuance of an act. Additionally, Parliament lacks competence in certain areas, external trade being one, while the Commission suffers no such weakness. In both cases, however, it is clear that Parliament has reached a degree of influence which makes it easier for both Council and Commission to consult with it rather than bypass it, circumstances permitting. The Amsterdam Summit and its grants of further power to Parliament only increases the likelihood of this happening (Earnshaw and Judge, 1996).

This, broadly, is the context in which the salience of Parliament becomes important for its electorate. MEPs can question Commissioners in Parliament but Commissioners do not face the electorate in any situation of genuine dialogue. If, as former President Delors conceded before leaving office, the union has evolved too quickly for its citizens to grasp, then the Parliament must become a vehicle for assisting the mobilisation of European voters.

Parliament and Media Relations

From its early years Parliament had a Press Office which provided facilities for mass media and through which journalists were accredited, press releases issued and interviews with Parliament officials were organised or facilitated. Documentation of the Parliament's activities was not a prime responsibility of the Press Office but it did provide some documentation and it was consulted on the format of some of the documentation produced elsewhere in the Secretariat.

First in the Assembly, and then in the early years of Parliament, meetings were relatively few and documentation relatively slight. There was a rudimentary network of field offices in member countries and no great pressure to make Parliament more salient for electorates in those countries. The Press Office was a small operation and a minor player on the Parliament stage.

The expansion of EU, and the popular election of MEPs in 1979, transformed the situation. A much enlarged, elected legislature with increased powers meant much more activity in party groups, parliamentary committees, plenary sessions – and media attention. The Press Office and its function expanded steadily through the 1970s and 1980s. Employees of DG III stood at 370 in 1997 of whom as many as 60 directly assisted journalists of all types. Given that Parliament met primarily in two sites – Strasbourg and Brussels – the costs of providing two sets of facilities for journalists was not small and, as with other aspects of Parliament, widely commented upon. By 1994, journalists who did not wish to follow Parliament to Strasbourg could access some of its proceedings in Brussels while documentation was eventually produced in both centres. Such journalists could not hold face to face interviews with MEPs during plenary sessions at Strasbourg. To encourage journalistic attendance at Strasbourg, Parliament provided financial assistance for reporters and, to its satisfaction, saw results. Average journalistic attendance increased by 75 per cent between 1990 and 1994, while the number of television reports increased by 40 per cent and hours of coverage tripled over the same period (Corbett, 1995, p. 298).

Until 1995 the Press Office was headed by Guido Naets, a distinguished former Belgian journalist. When interviewed before his retirement, he claimed that one of the greatest difficulties of the Office was the way some Commissioners, and representatives of member governments, demeaned Parliament in the eyes of journalists, at times encouraging them to treat it with indifference, even contempt.

The Press Office operates in the full awareness that it is not the principal source of information for journalists. MEPs, party spokespersons, national delegations and committee staffs – all are competitors. It follows that a significant part of the office's activities lies in trying to harmonise the flow of information by filling information gaps, correcting errors and countering misinformation. Office staff are well aware that, at individual and party levels, Parliament as an institution is misrepresented by its own members for personal, partisan, national and ideological purposes. Like its Congressional counterpart in Washington the institution, qua institution, is a target for internal hostilities and becomes a cause to oppose in itself. The Office therefore has to walk a tightrope between institutional, party, national and individual pressures.

The field offices in member countries can represent a further source of difficulty. Where news of Parliament concerns one member country particularly, it is accepted that the local field office will lead on its media and public presentation. Both the Commission and Parliament, for example, accept that agreed press releases will be issued one hour earlier in the country concerned and have to accept a degree of 'national spin' put on it by the field office. As with the Commission, so with Parliament, there has to be an acceptance, albeit reluctantly, that a decision on a policy is presented as a 'victory' for one member and a defeat for others. The Press Office and the Secretariat generally have to work within what is perceived as this inevitable, if sometimes deplorable, situation.

3 The European Parliament, Members, Issues

Tappin put together a multinational effort and showed that EU could work (Commission Official, 1995).

MEPs – Roles, Conflicts, Choices

The European Parliament sits within a system which exhibits some significant similarities to the US federal system – or appears to be developing such similarities. Subsidiarity has a variety of definitions but all include all-Union and local government arenas with that of the middle tier – national governments within the EU – being the more problematic level of responsibility to define (Andersen and Eliasssen, 1996). The Parliament, with its limited area of legislative competence, has to be mindful of all three levels and its members, some of whom are members of either national or local legislatures, behave accordingly.

In the British case the situation is made more complicated by the constituency system which means that MEPs have to satisfy the demands of both party and constituency at home and cross-party groupings in Brussels and Strasbourg. Since no party list protects them, constituency survival has to be their top priority where their majorities are not large. Thus, despite party systems which are generally much more dominant than in the US, British MEPs have much in common with American legislators. In their first term they must secure their electoral survival and, thereafter, pursue party and career advance in a variety of legislative arenas. Hence, like their American counterparts, they have to cultivate a 'home style' – a public persona and pattern of behaviour which meets the various demands made on their positions. In his classic 1978 study of members of Congress Richard Fenno distinguished three arenas of decision for a member, namely the use of resources, 'presentation of self,' and choice of strategic political themes. The first, he said, involved decisions over the allocation of personal time and staff resources; the second involved decisions over face-to-face relationships with groups and individuals in the constituency; while the third related to choices of political themes or postures. In the case of Congress the latter might involve running as a 'Liberal' or 'Conservative' or 'running against Congress and Washington' or steering clear of party and group affinities – being a 'loner' or 'maverick'.

Fenno's typology cannot be simply applied to MEPs (Fenno, 1978) but it is suggestive despite the differences which the traditionally more ideological and disciplined British party structures publicly allow. That having been said, the British system does not preclude, indeed expects, individual MPs to decide on resource allocation and personal presentation matters especially in marginal seats. Even in the choice of strategic themes British party 'lines' can and do change and MEPs must be allowed flexibility of political emphasis. Scots and Welsh MEPs cannot avoid elements of cross party 'national' activities while, in England, regional emphases jostle with ideological factionalism, generational differences and localism in all parties. Thus the individual MEP has to make many of the choices made by his or her US counterpart and makes these choices in the increasingly transnational milieu of Euro-wide groupings.

European Parliament constituencies in the UK can cover as many as eight Westminster constituencies. With far-flung electorates appropriate uses of mass media are doubly important. Reaching large electorates calls for as much media exposure as possible as MEPs are only too well aware. The difficulties are, of course, obvious. Newspapers, broadly, work in vertically or horizontally stratified markets and tend to keep within their boundaries. Thus the national press concentrates on national stories and only touches regional or local news where it perceives a direct national interest. In turn local newspapers assume that readers see a national or big regional newspaper and concentrate on local news or news of politics and policies having a local resonance. Radio and television, likewise, have technical or market created notions of regions and behave accordingly in all their news and not merely the political.

European news, therefore, has to compete in an arena which is crowded and in which Euro-news has to be given a direct national or local referent. MEPs are only too well aware that EU news in the UK is given no cachet simply because it is EU news. Further MEPs are aware that political partisanship within and between media will constrain judgements of news relevance while, equally, audience partisanship plays a significant role in news choice.

16 *The European Parliament, Mass Media and the Search for Power and Influence*

An MEP's 'home style' cannot avoid these moulding influences. Large 'safe' majorities, good local party organisations, a well disposed set of local newspapers and radio and television reporters hungry for Euro-news of local and regional relevance; all can make for one kind of 'style' while the absence of one or more such factors can frame a contrasting 'style'. Seniority, public visibility at national level, identification with an issue of particular constituency significance, the rise and fall in the popularity of the national party; all contribute to the 'style' of a sitting MEP. Equally important, the increasing salience of the EU and the rising volume of constituency service activities make large contributions. In all these senses MEPs are little different from their Westminster counterparts. There is, however, the crucial factor of historic familiarity with the national system and an absence of this for European institutions and, perhaps particularly, for the European Parliament.

MEPs have to be highly selective in their legislative specialisms and, at least until their party nominations are secure, have to concentrate on constituency matters and imperatives. Inevitably some MEPs are rarely available for wider party tasks and thus find their advance within Parliament frustratingly slow. MEPs, unlike MPs, enjoy little or no deference. Indeed some have to endure xenophobic sentiments from constituents who accuse them of having 'gone native'.

MEPs – Work Weeks, Staffs and Routines

Technically the European Parliament is in session for 44 weeks a year. Eleven of these weeks are spent in plenary sessions in Strasbourg and the remaining weeks in Brussels focusing on committee, party and group activities. One week a month the Parliament Secretariat, MEPs and at least one or two of their staff members decamp to Strasbourg where, in addition to plenary sessions, further committee and group meetings take place.

An MEP's work life has to be built around this framework. The average British MEP has two offices – one mostly Brussels-based and one in the constituency. The £83K expenses the MEP receives is expected to cover the costs of running both offices – paying for salaries, office rent, telephones, faxes and stationery in Brussels and Strasbourg. The average MEP usually employs two full-timers in the Brussels and constituency offices, and supplements these with part-timers. The full-timers are the linchpins of the office operation handling not only routine constituency and party business but, frequently, acting as policy researchers for the MEP and liaising with the staffs of the member's committees and other formal and informal groups. In their constituency offices some Labour MEPs have placed one or more family members on the payroll but, of late, this has attracted increasing Party criticism and pressure. The part-timers in Brussels may be drawn from a growing pool of political workers who are Brussels based and looking for Commission, Parliament or other EU related jobs, for example with lobbyists or consultancy partnerships. Sometimes, additionally, the Brussels office may have a British university student – usually following a European Studies course – who will be registered at a Belgian university and gain credits for the office work they do for MEPs. Often such students have Brussels ambitions and will be looking for civil service opportunities after they graduate. Given their language competencies they can make a significant addition to mostly monoglot English-speaking offices.

The constituency office will, as mentioned, have its full- and part-timers and intermittent assistance from unpaid party activists. With a boss who is away four days in most weeks its work relies heavily on the directing full-time aide from Monday to Thursday and focuses on a tightly scheduled set of activities on Fridays and Saturdays when the MEP is present. There is a heavy component of letter writing, both to initiate activity and elicit information for the MEP. Examples here would be letters to local and central government or local and national professional and business organisations. Constituent queries cover a wide range of issues some of which are outside the jurisdiction of the European Parliament. Some of these are referred back to MPs and more on to other appropriate recipients. Staff can draft queries and replies but the MEP has to be involved in finalising all but the most low level correspondence and telephone and fax follow ups.

For the MEP a typical Brussels work day might look like:

8:30a.m. – 9:00a.m. Correspondence and briefings. Telephone calls.

9:00a.m. – 12:30p.m. Committee or Group meetings.

12:30p.m. – 1:00p.m. Private meeting with an MEP or lobbyist. Telephone calls.

1:00p.m. – 2:30p.m. Working lunch with representatives of business and professional groups. Informal MEP meetings – visitors.

2:30p.m. – 6:30p.m.   A Committee or Party task force meeting.

6:30p.m. – 7:00p.m.   Clear mail and telephone calls. Set up timetable for the following day.

7:30p.m.   A reception given by outside organisations seeking to interest MEPs and acquire public visibility.

In Strasbourg there are intergroup meetings and the very large addition of the need to attend and speak in plenary sessions. The work week in Strasbourg begins on Monday afternoon and, mostly, is over by Thursday evening. MEPs can draw the attendance allowance of £170 on Friday morning and then depart for Brussels or home, a fact critically reported in a recent British television documentary. In both Brussels and Strasbourg the picture is mostly similar – that is, too many meetings interspersed with the treadmill of telephone calls, faxes and letters. The time for researching a topic of real interest is usually too short, hence the reliance of MEPs on staff for both their legislative and constituency matters. This reliance is not always recognised by adequate remuneration so that recently there has been an increasing degree of staff agitation and turnover.

Equally important for the constituency office is the organising of the Friday and weekend meetings. The range of these can be very wide – MEPs see individual constituents, spokespersons of all kinds, local councillors, party officials, journalists and so on. A not untypical Friday or Saturday appointments list might look like:

Friday

9:15a.m. – 10:30a.m.   Deal with mail and see one or two constituents. Telephone calls.

11:00a.m. – noon   See council officials to progress a local bid for European funds or frame a request for legislation.

12:30p.m. – 2:30p.m.   Working lunch with local company or industry group. Telephone calls.

3:00p.m. – 4:30p.m.   Visit local school, college or company to meet staff, students and employees, etc. Make short speech.

4:45p.m. – 5:30p.m.   Back to office to clear mail and other business.

7:30p.m. – 10:30p.m. Be present at a Dinner for party or local organisation. Make speech.

Saturday
9:15a.m. – 11:00a.m. See individual constituents. Further briefings and telephone calls.

11:00a.m. – 2:00p.m. Tour part of constituency and end with a working lunch with Party or local organisations. Make speech and, perhaps, arrange a future visit to Brussels or Strasbourg.

Whether working out of Brussels or the constituency office MEPs have more to do than they are comfortable with. The future promises no relief as Parliament becomes more significant. Members have to work their staffs ever harder and turnover is high. Despite their best efforts almost all complain that developing their legislative interests is difficult, a situation which makes them feel overly dependent on Party staff or, worse, on Commission officials. Constituency and party pressures, one noted, keep them busy but, as in the US Congress, too often on the wrong things (Davidson and Oleszek, 1990). The difficulties inherent in working in a multilingual Parliament with multinational groupings, components of which can have very different policy priorities reflective of national situations, are only too obvious.

A Case Study – Ceramics, China and the European Parliament

MEPs have to understand, harmonise and defend the vital interests of their constituencies. In political systems where there is no strong constituency dimension within the representation process, then national parties have to be the vehicle for that task. In Germany MEPs can be regional MPs and, in France, local mayors. Elsewhere there may be a voluntary relationship with a locality within the larger constituency. But in all such systems the defence of local interests has to be within the party hierarchy. In Belgium and Ireland, for example, the principal vehicle for the defence of interests will, in the first instance, be the party hierarchy and its relationship with the bureaucracy and, if the party is out of power, with the governing coalition. In the UK party is a very important dimension and may well determine whether an interest will be successfully defended. That having been said, however, the territorial dimension makes it incumbent on MPs and MEPs to be prime movers in the process. For both, there is an element of Parliamentary 'courtesy' which inhibits representatives from taking the lead in a problem primarily the concern of a colleague's constituency, or group of constituencies. The ceramics case illuminates this clearly.

Historically the ceramics industry, in all its forms, became principally located in Stoke on Trent. The Six Towns (Hanley, Burslem, Stoke, etc.) have dominated the industry for more than a century. Names such as Wedgwood, Royal Minton, and Royal Doulton products became internationally known and their prestige extended to more recent ceramic industrial products. The industry gave Stoke a counter-cyclical economy employing a large share of the workforce and, with relatively high wages, providing a large share of local income. Decades of foreign competition have pushed local producers out of the mass market and into the high value sector both for domestic and overseas markets. The industry, though losing 18,000 jobs over the last decade, continues to employ 15 per cent of the local workforce and is a mainstay of the local economy. Entry in the EU had allowed it to expand into European markets, hitherto well protected, for both domestic and industrial products and the industry looked forward to a healthy future marketing traditional and new product lines. The merger of Wedgwood and the German Rosenthal company symbolised this confidence.

After 1993, however, the industry became growingly concerned over non-EU competition, particularly from China and the Far East. China was not only a serious competitor in the traditional domestic product market, but also seemed bent on securing a growing share in the market for industrial ceramics. Given its labour cost advantage, its new plants and increasing research and development budgets China, it was clear, could put Stoke out of business. Little wonder that representations were promptly made to the Thatcher government on the question of lower quotas within the World Trade Organisation and EU regulations. The latter, particularly, was identified as the key arena since other EU producers had an interest.

Trade Commissioner Sir Leon Brittan, a free trade believer, was not sympathetic. He had to be evenhanded between EU ceramics' industries and, even more, had to bear in mind the overall balance of trade possibilities with China, potentially a huge market for EU goods and one already deeply penetrated by the US and Japan. Under Brittan's guidance the EU sought not to be seen as 'parochial' about one industry and must not be seen in that way about one country. As with other threatened industries within EU the balance of advantage was not easily struck and usually difficult to defend before any one member government.

Precisely for this reason the Parliament's intervention became significant. It had no formal jurisdiction over EU external trade, the terms of which were the responsibility of the Commission and the Council of Ministers. Parliament, however, wished to enlarge its jurisdiction and members made regular representations to the Commission. When these came from the larger parties in the legislature they could not be ignored. It was in this context that Michael Tappin, Labour MEP for Staffordshire West and Congleton, became a significant player in the Parliament and the larger arena.

Tappin, a first term MEP, had had a long history of effective Labour Party activities at local level. His sprawling constituency, inevitably, had areas of internal political tensions which were reflected in the differing political representations at Westminster. The rural and Tory-leaning areas were potentially in conflict with the interests of the industrial centres such as Stoke and Stafford. The latter towns themselves were both allies and rivals. While Stoke was a pottery town, Stafford was a heavy engineering centre dominated by the General Electric-Alsthom Company. The histories and the microcultures of all three areas were different and Tappin was well aware that accusations of 'favouritism' came easily from some important Labour actors, to say nothing of local Tory leaders. The MEP, a former Keele University lecturer in American Government, had to show that he could be effective in EU matters, that he could, as Americans would say 'bring home the bacon' for his constituency without losing political capital elsewhere. There had, in short, to be a harmonisation of parties in local government and Westminster constituencies. Tappin needed bipartisanship to ensure that his Parliamentary activities would be supplemented by British government pressures in the 113 Committee which reported to the Council. From the outset, therefore, he had to work to find common ground between disparate interests and political rivals and had to seek a 'constituency persona' which was above a mere party identity. Successful defence of the ceramics industry was not only an imperative for political survival but, as he saw, could be the means of establishing himself as 'Mr Europe' a vital component of long term effectiveness, both locally and in the Parliament.

If bipartisanship was the watchword at home, then self-promotion and hard work in Parliament had to be the equivalents. Tappin was fortunate in being an energetic member of the largest national contingent in the European Socialist Party, the majority in the European Parliament. To begin he had first to sensitise the Parliament, Commission, Council – and the industry – to the real dangers facing the British ceramics industry. This meant involving fellow MEPs from member countries, even when they represented interests which rivalled those of Stoke. The latter meant appealing to a common attachment both to EU solutions, and pragmatic considerations. Hence, from the beginning of his campaign in 1994, he secured a detailed flow of industrial information on Chinese competition and on its methods and effects. He then used this to persuade first British and then other colleagues, of its general significance for the UK and EU. He was, of course, working within a favourable general environment since the EU was resisting 'sweatshop' competition from the Third World, and pressures from the US in the then all-encompassing World Trade Organisation (WTO) negotiations. Precisely because of this, however, the problems of one industry had to fight to be heard among competing interests of Brussels and Strasbourg. Tappin's local government and American knowledge gave him some advantages over some British colleagues working for other sectors. Assiduous work in the Labour Group and elsewhere in the Parliament led to the establishment of the Ceramics Intergroup which offset the fact that the European Socialist Party leadership was divided on Tappin's campaign. A strongly worded petition was presented to the Commission and Council of Ministers and, at every stage, all constituency media and the UK delegation were kept informed and remained supportive.

The question of limiting Chinese quotas was not a simple one since EU countries had a growing trading relationship in China and, in some cases were rivals within the Chinese market. Even if the Ceramics Intergroup was on his side, Tappin knew that the Commission needed more pressure and persuasion to give the ceramics problem the higher profile it needed. By careful bipartisan consultations locally and at Westminster, Tappin kept potentially disparate interests in harmony amidst a whirlwind of similar pleas from other sectors. By late 1995 the Commission had accepted the need for action and, by early 1996, the Chinese faced a significantly changed quota bargaining position, somewhat to their chagrin. Tappin and his allies, however, knew that they had to continue to demonstrate that the European ceramics industries were increasingly efficient, innovative and competitive and not merely seeking to hide behind an EU tariff wall, and that task has to be ongoing.

Tappin's success, seen at constituency and Parliament level, was recognised as a considerable political achievement. He had demonstrated personal effectiveness at all levels and, additionally, the crucial significance of European-wide action. The EU could be shown to have worked for his constituency, the Labour Party and the new MEP. A local ceramics producer noted that 'some other EU producers could be relaxed about the Chinese, but we couldn't and he saved our bacon'. A Dutch MEP observed that 'Tappin put together a multinational effort and showed that EU worked'.

Conclusions

British MEPs find themselves in a difficult and, for many members, a novel situation. The Parliament's style is coalitional not adversarial and, as in the US Congress, members are expected to help write legislation often of a complex, lengthy nature. Specialisation of interest among members is the norm, real expertise commands respect and, occasionally deference. Speeches in plenaries and contributions in committees are tightly controlled by chairs who oppose 'sloganeering'. Members are expected to think on a European-wide basis, and it is expected that national interests will be declared. Members themselves have to decide on their self-presentation, political personae and priorities. It is a busy, novel experience in a different milieu generating, as one member noted, a 'schizoid tendency when I have to mix my Brussels and local style'. Many British MEPs from all parties confess to finding this different context not wholly unacceptable. Indeed, some are frank to say that any Westminster ambitions they may have had have faded considerably. While the travel and work load are undoubtedly tiring, the job itself is appealing, not to say very rewarding. For many members British party politics seem decreasingly attractive. That, however, does not mean that they are happy with Parliamentary ways and even less with the powers of Parliament vis-à-vis Commission and Council. Currently, among Labour members, this unhappiness is being overlain by the fear of Labour Party imposed 'deselection' via the mechanism of the party list. More than ever this puts a premium on being effective – and loyal. On all fronts media exposure of the right kind is necessary and it is to this that we now turn.

4 British News Coverage of the European Union

Information is a key variable in the process of creating an image of political institutions and processes. Hence the volume and quality of that information is crucial. The European Union (EU) has every reason to wish to assess the coverage it receives and, until recently, routinely surveyed EU news in member countries. Each month Directorate General X is in receipt of the Euromedia Survey which charts the previous month's coverage of a broad range of newspaper, magazine and television stories on EU in all 15 member countries (Euromedia, February–November, 1996). Coverage is analysed in quantitative and qualitative terms – the latter being primarily concerned to measure pro or anti-EU 'tendencies'.

Table 4.1 provides the Euromedia data on issue coverage for the period February to November 1996. It was a period when, with the British election pending, British media were much concerned by tension in the Conservative Party over European Monetary Union, the BSE crisis, the Bosnian crisis and future relations with NATO. Together these represented major news stories for mass media in all member countries and it would have been surprising if there had not been considerable media coverage of them. Analysis of this data is interesting in several ways. Over the whole period the distribution of British press coverage was not much different from that of the EU average. On the key issue areas, the total volume of UK coverage, as elsewhere, increased steadily so that the EU average monthly figure for the last three months of the survey showed a more than 50 per cent increase over that for the first three months. EU news became steadily more salient for media and audiences.

If the UK coverage is disaggregated the pattern of national media concerns is clear. Despite an expectation that BSE news would predominate, British media coverage did not reflect this except on television. As the Dublin Summit approached questions relating to the general evolution of EU, especially in economic matters, were more covered. In both cases British media coverage was noticeably higher on average than that of EU

Table 4.1 Press coverage of EU issue areas in 15 member states, February–November 1996 %

Issue areas		Feb. n = 6455	Mar. n = 8418	Apr. n = 6103	May n = 7842	June n = 8275	July n = 8544	Aug. n = 6015	Sept. n = 9193	Oct. n = 12820	Nov. n = 10114	UK av.	EU av.
Economic and financial	EU	21.7	16.2	21.9	19.1	15.2	17.6	20.6	25.3	26.4	27.2		21.1
	UK	17.3	23.9	21.4	16.6	13.9	25.1	21.5	33.9	32.3	30.4	23.6	
EU development	EU	18.3	24.2	8.9	20.4	18.9	14.0	16.9	17.2	20.4	15.5		17.5
	UK	31.1	24.9	20.4	17.6	30.1	17.8	23.0	19.8	29.2	18.6	23.3	
EU foreign policy	EU	14.6	13.9	9.4	9.7	7.2	13.1	14.4	9.0	11.6	11.9		11.5
	UK	9.5	14.16	6.5	5.3	4.2	9.9	10.4	6.6	9.6	7.2	8.3	
EU institutions	EU	9.2	6.4	4.7	5.9	13.5	8.6	6.7	8.0	8.1	6.1		7.7
	UK	5.8	4.9	4.8	4.9	8.9	5.9	2.0	4.2	4.6	6.9	5.3	
EU social, health and employment policies	EU	8.4	10.8	11.6	8.6	8.4	6.1	5.0	6.1	5.5	7.5		7.8
	UK	10.9	8.2	14.8	9.7	7.5	9.5	7.3	7.7	5.9	18.8	10.0	
EU agricultural policy	EU	4.2	9.8	13.9	14.0	15.5	10.3	6.7	8.5	5.1	4.9		9.3
	UK	10.5	5.9	18.9	12.6	23.2	12.0	12.3	12.5	5.6	4.1	11.7	

and, of course, was mostly devoted to concerns over possibly unwelcome outcomes. BSE news, nevertheless, recorded a 20 per cent higher average than that for EU but so, too, did the coverage of matters concerned with the consequences of the Maastricht Treaty – the so-called Social Chapter. EU institutions as such appeared to be less covered on average in the UK – intermittent coverage of unwelcome Commission or Court decisions was the norm. Finally, the coverage of foreign policy matters was significantly less than the EU average. Despite a large troop commitment to Bosnia, UK coverage seemed less bothered by EU failure to play a decisive role there. This was probably owed to British government briefings which stressed that the Bosnian crisis justified British trust, not in the UN or EU, but in NATO, so far as foreign policy was concerned. EU efforts to create an alternative to NATO were officially frowned on and press coverage mostly reflected this posture. Overall EU news profiles, the UK included, were faithful reflections of the differing emphases of member governments.

Table 4.2 gives the Euromedia data for British press coverage of EU institutions and the Intergovernmental Conference (IGC) of 1996. The EU average monthly figures reveal the overall increase referred to above and the episodic quality of coverage. The Court, for example, was very visible in the first three months of the period and much less so in the last three months. The Commission coverage did not exhibit such a sharp contrast but did show a 30 per cent average monthly increase in coverage after the summer of 1996. Even more striking over the same period was the more than 100 per cent increase in coverage of the Parliament. Taken over the whole period Parliament secured the most coverage, being challenged only by that given to the multiple, but related, topics of the IGC, the Council of Ministers, and the newsworthy Presidency. Comparable UK data on these areas will be discussed later. For the moment it is worth noting that the volume of news of Parliament is noticeable. Volume, however, may not be the criterion of significance.

Newspaper profiles were mirrored in television coverage but, given the medium, more starkly. As Table 4.3 reveals the contrast between UK and EU averages was very noticeable. The BSE crisis illustrates this – UK coverage being several times greater than that in EU. Obviously that crisis was most significant for the British; television coverage was much greater and heavily entangled with voter concerns over the government's responsibility for the original policy. The coverage illuminates British attitudes to EU membership generally. On foreign policy questions the mixture of pro-NATO, and lower anxiety levels over Bosnia, was clear with EU coverage

Table 4.2 Press coverage of European Union institutions, February–November 1996 %

EU institution	Feb.	Mar.	Apr.	May	June	July	Aug.	Sept.	Oct.	Nov.	EU av.
Court	25	27	27	21	5	11	6	–	3	6	13.1
Commission	24	16	10	11	6	17	31	21	18	25	17.9
Parliament	15	21	17	20	0	13	37	31	56	25	23.5
Council of Ministers EU Presidency/IGC	16	11	19	24	61	23	14	25	10	22	22.5

Table 4.3 Monthly averages for television coverage, February–November 1996 %

Issue area	UK average	EU average
Foreign policy	2.9	14.9
Economic, financial	22.4	18.4
EU development	14.8	12.7
Employment, social	4.4	7.5
Justice and internal	0.0	3.0
Admin. matters	0.0	0.8
EU institutions	3.4	3.9
Agricultural	38.5	15.2
Fisheries	1.3	0.0
Competition	0.0	3.4

of Bosnia generally being four times that seen on British television. Similarly EU averages on employment and social matters, as well as competition law, were noticeably higher than those in the UK.

The contrasts become more meaningful when these total are disaggregated as in Table 4.4. Comparing pre- and post-summer figures, British coverage of EU development, institutions and fishery policies go down noticeably while coverage of social and agricultural policies go up, the latter from an already high figure. Coverage of agriculture, in fact, is almost as large as all other categories combined. The BSE crisis and its consequences were clearly stories that fitted television news values – tragedy, government incompetence, failures among experts and hints of both a government and EU 'cover up'.

The monthly Euromedia survey was a valuable research tool and the termination of its monitoring by the Commission is much to be regretted. The period chosen by the author was, of course, limited from February through November 1996. It is accepted that, in its wide selection of printed

British News Coverage of the European Union 29

Table 4.4 Television coverage – UK and 5 EU countries, February–November 1996 %

Issue area		Feb.	Mar.	Apr.	May	June	July	Aug.	Sept.	Oct.	Nov.	Monthly averages UK	Monthly averages EU
n =	EU	343	860	654	550	785	315	308	410	560	479		
	UK	20	63	61	37	91	18	12	36	35	55		
Foreign policy	EU	24.0	13.0	12.0	11.0		11.0	28.0	12.0	19.0	19.0	2.9	14.9
	UK	12.0								17.0			
Economic and financial	EU	17.0	9.0	13.0	16.0	21.0	18.0	6.0	27.0	22.0	35.0	22.4	18.3
	UK	53.0	18.0	19.0			44.0		19.0	23.0	48.0		
EU development	EU	13.0	20.0	12.0	18.0	12.0	6.0		12.0	17.0	16.0	12.7	14.0
	UK	18.0	23.0	18.0	14.0	28.0				30.0	17.0		
Employment, health and social policy	EU	9.0	14.0	12.0	17.0		7.0	7.0	9.0		17.0	2.7	9.2
	UK			11.0	8.0			8.0					
Justice and international affairs	EU	8.0	7.0					7.0	8.0				3.0
	UK												
Administrative matters	EU	8.0											0.8
	UK												
EU institutions	EU	6.0	4.0			15.0	9.0	5.0				3.4	3.9
	UK					26.0		8.0					
Agricultural policy	EU		21.0	25.0	20.0	18.0	25.0	15.0	20.0	11.0		38.5	13.0
	UK		42.0	40.0	72.0	43.0		83.0	53.0	27.0			
Fisheries	EU						22.0					1.3	2.2
	UK						13.0						
Competition policy	EU						11.0	23.0					2.4
	UK												

sources, and its analysis only of BBC television coverage, the Euromedia data might misrepresent the coverage common to a majority of voters. Thus there was need for supplementary data on both press and television and Tables 4.5–4.9 provide data independently derived from content analysis done as part of the Liverpool Project (DGX, 1996.)

Table 4.5 presents the data based on BBC 9p.m. and ITV 10p.m. news programmes – commanding the largest audience – for the summer and autumn months. As the left hand columns show stories relating to any aspect of EU are frequent – averaging nearly one every other day before August and more in the autumn. The BBC runs more stories than ITV though this data does not allow comparison of the time given to each story. This difference is almost certainly the outcome of a decision by ITV editors after 1992 to concentrate on a domestically oriented news agenda (Pilling, 1994). There are, however, some difficulties in analysing EU news at this time. To begin, there is the problem of disentangling EU from European news, a problem made more difficult because EU news often appeared in the Business sections of newspapers and made the main news section only when linked to stories covering Conservative Party stresses and Labour exploitation of these.

These cautions having been noted, however, certain observations can be made. In terms of mentions of Europe 70 per cent refer to Europe under a variety of headings – nation states, economic policy, foreign and defence policy etc. Some 20 per cent, however, do relate specifically to EU matters and difficulties. Further, it is possible to identify aspects of EU or Europe as news areas. The principal foci are the Commission, the European Court and the European Court of Human Rights. The European Parliament and the Council of Ministers, by comparison, receive little or no coverage. Thus for viewers EU is symbolised by a Commission which is subordinate to a Council of Ministers from member states and, often, a Court which is not a constituent part of EU. This picture may be more distorted than normal by the BSE crisis. It must be said, however, that British television coverage of EU is not so much infrequent as less than informative on EU's structures and their outcomes.

Examining the leading broadsheet and tabloid newspaper coverage gives a somewhat different picture. As Table 4.6 shows both types of newspapers provided a great deal of information in their 'newsholes' – more than two-thirds of their space on average. Of course that space has to cover all social, political and economic information. This is the context of all EU news and, within that news of the European Parliament. Table 4.7 provides

Table 4.5 BBC 9p.m. and ITN 10p.m. news coverage, May–November 1996*

		Stories		Mentions				
	Source	No. of dates	No. of EU stories	EU	European – general	EP/MEP	European Commission	Council of Ministers	European Court	Total mentions

	Source	No. of dates	No. of EU stories	EU	European – general	EP/MEP	European Commission	Council of Ministers	European Court	Total mentions
May	BBC	13	17	25	89	1	12	0	9	136
	ITN	13	16	21	81	0	7	0	3	112
June	BBC	15	23	37	85	3	10	1	7	143
	ITN	14	16	14	55	1	4	0	2	76
July	BBC	6	10	9	20	2	3	0	1	35
	ITN	4	5	3	26	0	2	0	0	31
Sept.	BBC	15	20	9	31	1	4	0	1	46
	ITN	15	18	15	56	0	1	1	7	80
Oct.	BBC	16	25	16	45	0	1	0	0	62
	ITN	12	14	3	31	0	3	0	1	38
Nov.	BBC	15	22	14	48	0	5	0	8	75
	ITN	10	12	9	31	1	0	0	6	47
Totals			198	175	598	9	52	2	45	881
Percentages				19.8%	67.9%	0.01%	5.9%	0.02%	5.1%	

* August excluded – Parliament in recess – EU vacation month.

Table 4.6 Average number of pages per newspaper, minus advertisements – selected newspapers

Newspaper	Pages average total	Pages/% average newshole
European	37.3	32.6 (87.4%)
Guardian	25.6	19.4 (75.8%)
Independent	28.2	20.9 (74.1%)
Times	51.6	40.0 (77.5%)
Financial Times	47.0	38.5 (81.9%)
Telegraph	40.5	30.0 (74.0%)
Averages	38.3	78.5
Express	88.0	62.2 (70.7%)
Mail	68.0	57.7 (84.8%)
Mirror	40.0	31.7 (79.3%)
Averages	65.3	78.3

Source: taken from 12 randomly-selected newspapers from the period 1 September to 31 November.

the breakdown of the latter. Nearly a third of the stories provided were political with the level of *Financial Times* coverage being noticeably above average. Inside that total, EU news averaged some 13 per cent of stories with, again, *Financial Times* coverage being noticeably higher. Once again, too, the average number of EU stories increased after August. Finally, within EU total news, stories focusing on the Parliament also increased sharply with the *Financial Times* coverage being noticeably down. The tabloid newspapers provided some contrast. From smaller 'newsholes' they provided on average a third of the number of political stories found in the broadsheets, only 10 per cent being EU stories but almost as many being devoted to the Parliament and the flow increased as the year wore on.

Table 4.7 Average daily number of news items, February–November 1996 – selected newspapers

Newspaper	News items	Political items	EU news items	EP news items
Guardian	70.9 (100%)	26.9 (37.9%)	3.1 *(11.5%)	0.23 *(0.85%)
Independent	67.5 (100%)	23.5 (34.8%)	3.1 *(13.2%)	0.25 *(1%)
Times	99.3 (100%)	31.3 (31.5%)	3.45 *(11%)	0.3 *(0.96%)
Financial Times	111.2 (100%)	44.4 (40%)	7.5 *(16.9%)	0.12 *(0.3%)
Telegraph	89.5 (100%)	29.6 (33%)	4.4 *(14.8%)	0.29 *(0.98%)
Averages		31.1	13.4	0.8
Express	42.2 (100%)	11.9 (28.2%)	1.5 *(12.6%)	0.12 *(1%)
Mail	48.6 (100%)	12 (24.7%)	1.9 *(15.8%)	0.08 *(0.6%)
Mirror	32.7 (100%)	6.9 (21.1%)	0.84 *(12.2%)	0 *(0%)
Averages		10.2	1.4	0.7

n% – percentage of news items daily
*(n%) – percentage of total political news

Averages, however, conceal considerable variations and some of these are significant in the context of the impact of news on audiences. To this end further data is now presented from the leading broadsheets and tabloid newspapers.

Tables 4.8 and 4.9 provide data on press coverage of EU and EP news in two contrasting periods during 1996. The first, May–July, was one in which the BSE crisis dominated British news of EU and one, too, when the British government position was defeated. The second, September–November, covers the period after that defeat when EU news was less dominated by only one question except insofar as EU membership and dissent in the Conservative Party threatened the survival of the Major government.

Tables 4.8a and 4.8b provide data on EU and EP coverage drawn from five broadsheet newspapers and three tabloids over the first of the two periods. The dominance of the European Commission and Council of Ministers originated news, and British responses, was clear providing as it did some three-quarters of the news items. Newspapers, with the exception of the Mirror, front paged EU news and, when such news appeared elsewhere in the newspaper it was mostly 'above the fold', that is in eye catching positions. Interestingly, news of the Parliament and its members was not insignificant accounting as it did for more than one-third of the mentions and, on average, being the second biggest news source.

Variations between newspapers reflect their ideological and , probably, market positions. Those hostile to EU – the *Times* and the *Telegraph* – front paged EU news heavily and were least prone among the broadsheets to put EU news 'below the fold'. The *Independent* was an exception here. Hostile newspapers, too, were most prone to highlight judgements of the European Court. The position of the *Financial Times* was that, having the large Brussels- and European-wide readership which it could not ignore, the newspaper gave qualified approval and heavy coverage to EU news. Newspapers with similar views – the *Guardian* and the *Independent* – front paged EU news more and gave more Parliament news in percentage terms.

When Parliament news, Table 4.8b, is examined for the first period some interesting points emerge. Only the *Times* gave front page status to Parliament news among the broadsheets. A higher proportion of Parliament news was below the fold but only in the *Independent* did this constitute a majority of items. In the *Financial Times*, the *Times* and the *Telegraph* the bulk of the items had an MEP as a focus for their news item. In the *Guardian* and *Independent* this was much less so, though both exceeded the broadsheet average in MEP letters. Once again the *Financial Times* was exceptional having the highest proportion of MEP news with 70 per cent being in the form of letters from MEPs. The *Daily Express* was exceptional in ignoring Parliament totally.

Turning to the second period (September–November), Tables 4.9a and 4.9b provide data which indicate some interesting contrasts. On average EU

British News Coverage of the European Union   35

Table 4.8a News items, European Union, May–July 1996 %

	n=7 FT	n=28 Telegraph	n=28 Guardian	n=30 Independent	n=24 Times	Broadsheet average	n=23 Mail	n=25 Express	n=11 Mirror	Tabloid average
Front page	35	29	31	17	54	33.2	13	16	–	10.7
Below fold	6	4	11	30	4	11.0	26	4	9	13.0
EP	47	46	7	10	13	24.6	4	8	9	7.0
MEP	18	7	18	7	8	11.6	–	–	–	0.0
EC	71	86	46	100	83	77.2	74	44	54	42.3
ECJ	–	18	–	17	29	12.8	–	4	9	4.3

Table 4.8b European Parliament, May–July 1996 %

	n=13 FT	n=7 Telegraph	n=17 Guardian	n=11 Independent	n=11 Times	Broadsheet average	n=3 Mail	n= Express	n=1 Mirror	Tabloid average
Front page	–	–	–	–	27	5.0	–	–	–	0.0
Below fold	38	29	47	73	18	41.0	67	–	100	56.7
MEP	85	71	47	45	100	69.6	67	–	100	56.7
MEP letter	69	14	41	36	9	33.8	67	–	100	56.7
EC	–	–	–	–	–	0	–	–	–	0.0

news, except in the *Times*, was less front paged and more likely to be found 'below the fold'. Commission and Council focused news continued to be the dominant component, while European Court news had more than doubled in quantity. Parliament/MEP news was down overall but still the second largest component of EU news. The *Times* continued to be the most ready to front page EU news while the *Telegraph* and the *Express* appeared most ready to cover the Parliament. The three newspapers were relatively hostile to Parliament's pretensions. The *Guardian* gave Parliament moderate coverage but less to MEPs, while the *Independent* did the reverse being second only to the *Daily Mail* in the proportion of its coverage given to MEPs as such.

When EP news is disaggregated it is clear that the cooling of the BSE story was not good for Parliamentary coverage. The average level of coverage was markedly down, as indicated above, with the *Times* and the *Telegraph* being ready to give MEPs coverage but unwilling to give much space to their letters. Whereas in the earlier period news of Parliament appeared in the context of EU news, in the second period this dimension was absent, almost as though Parliament news had come of age. The *Guardian* and *Independent* gave reduced coverage with the former publishing fewer MEP letters but giving more MEP coverage, while the latter gave less of both kinds of news though giving twice as much space to MEP letters. Among the tabloids coverage was very slight though in total up sharply in the *Daily Mail*. The *Financial Times* was down, both on general and letter coverage, though front paging Parliament news and carrying much more Commission related news than other newspapers.

The crisis of the first period caused an increase in EU coverage, including that of the Parliament. That increase, however, predated the spring of 1996 and continued through the rest of the year. The BSE crisis highlighted the growing power not of EU institutions, so much as that of the integrated market, with Germany especially being a market the UK simply couldn't lose. The increase in volume was important for public awareness while the tone adopted reflected and sharpened popular tensions over EU membership and, ultimately, helped undermine the Major government.

To judge by the foregoing data those newspapers who saw themselves as pro EU generally responded to the crisis by giving not more EU coverage absolutely, but rather by giving MEPs more space. Conversely those newspapers who resented EU lectures on BSE increased the space given to EU news, but certainly not to Parliament or its members. Meanwhile the tabloid newspapers increased their coverage but still, overall, gave little room to EU news and virtually none to Parliament news. The pro-EU *Daily*

British News Coverage of the European Union 37

Table 4.9a News items, European Union, September–November 1996 %

	n=29 FT	n=24 Telegraph	n=24 Guardian	n=30 Independent	n=23 Times	n=23 Broadsheet average	n=23 Mail	n=25 Express	n=12 Mirror	Tabloid average
Front page	21	38	25	20	48	30.4	13	16	18	15.6
Below fold	3	4	14	37	17	15.0	26	8	17	17.0
EP	31	63	15	7	7	24.6	13	36	8	19.0
MEP	–	4	3	10	9	5.2	13	8	8	9.6
EC	90	83	71	87	74	81.0	100	68	58	75.3
ECJ	24	21	25	30	39	27.8	39	24	–	21.0

Table 4.9b European Parliament, September–November 1996 %

	n=23 FT	n=32 Telegraph	n=16 Guardian	n=32 Independent	n=27 Times	n=27 Broadsheet average	n=18 Mail	n=6 Express	n=1 Mirror	Tabloid average
Front page	21	–	–	3	4	5.6	6	–	–	2.0
Below fold	36	22	13	28	11	22.0	22	50	–	24.0
MEP	50	41	56	63	48	51.6	6	50	100	52.0
MEP letter	32	16	13	31	11	20.6	–	–	–	0.0
EC	36	9	13	9	22	17.8	22	17	–	13.0

Mirror gave little space to Parliament – one item in each period – though it increased its EU coverage. The *Daily Mail* and *Daily Express* substantially increased their EU coverage. The *Express* indeed by the autumn of 1996 had more Parliament coverage than any of the other papers. It was not, however, coverage which that institution appreciated.

5 British Newspapers and EU News

If Members ... criticise the standards of the Commission and member governments, they cannot go on as they are (Official in Parliament President's office, 1996).

The credibility of the Union is crumbling away (Gijs de Vries MEP, 1996).

Aggregate data, while critical for assessing the volume, frequency and profile of news between newspapers and countries, can only be a part of the story. To appreciate fully the impact or otherwise of European Union news it is necessary to sample what that news looked like to its readers. British attitudes toward the European Union were moulded heavily by media coverage which, by 1996, reflected in part the unity of the Labour Opposition and the disunity of the Conservative Party and government on questions relating to European integration. What news of EU institutions and policy appeared in different newspapers, how was it framed and how persuasive? All were crucial questions and to them we now turn.

The second quarter of 1996 was dominated by the BSE crisis and this could be said to have distorted the coverage. Certainly the crisis boosted EU coverage and in ways which revealed the range of doubts and hostilities toward European matters visible at elite and mass levels. Eurosceptics in the Tory Party had a field day as did their Labour counterparts, though in their case unattributably quoted. The mix of xenophobia, national bewilderment at the catastrophe facing the beef industry and the ignorance of EU attempts to assist the UK were plainly visible. EU news might be relatively infrequent but was clearly 'hot news' in this period. Of the newspapers in this sample only the *Financial Times* and the *Independent* could be said to give a favourable though not uncritical portrayal of EU events. The other newspapers were more critical, sometimes decidedly so. The coverage they gave suggested that EU events were only news if they held the EU up either to criticism or ridicule. A sample of the stories and presentation is all that can be given here.

The BSE story framed other stories. In late May the *Times* tied the story to the proposed cuts in fish quotas which the UK government proposed to resist (*Times*, May 31). The *Telegraph* a few days earlier had reported Commissioner Kinnock's reservations on the folly of the UK policy of non-cooperation and carried the views of three MEPs to that effect (*Telegraph*, 23 May). The following day the newspaper noted that Conservative MEPs were against British government policy (24 May) and 10 days later attacked their leader, Lord Plumb, and other MEPs as 'pro-German' (3 June). By contrast the *Independent* treated the matter in a much cooler fashion concentrating on EU's proposed assistance toward the costs of a large cull of British cattle. The newspaper assembled a collage of items from the anti-EU press, broadsheet and tabloid, under the title of 'The press crusade for a narrow nationalism'. In this the *Sun*, among other things, called for the abolition of the Parliament and advised the Parliament President who was 'nothing more than a jumped up civil servant ... to shut up' (*Sun*, 23 and 27 May; *Independent*, 3 June).

The *Financial Times* eschewed hysteria and by late July carried news of a briefing by Lord Plumb. In this he accused British civil servants of overzealous rule-making, the result of which was a prolongation of the BSE crisis through a lack of abattoir facilities. The piece ended with a source in Conservative Central Office dismissing this criticism in condescending fashion. 'It's pretty lonely being a Tory MEP and they sometimes feel marginalised in the modern Conservative Party. From time to time they make a song and dance about things', he said (*Financial Times*, 27 July). So much for the significance of a popularly elected European Parliament!

News of that Parliament was often portrayed very unsympathetically. In May the press story line appeared to be the cost of 'junkets' for MEPs, while on 22 May the *Telegraph* ran a story on MEP allowances tying that information to the high cost of Parliament buildings under construction in Brussels and Strasbourg (*Telegraph*, 22 May). Both stories were framed in a clear 'gravy train' mode with heavy emphasis on the rivalries between member states. On 4 June, however, the *Independent* carried a letter from Graham Watson MEP which attacked the newspaper for advocating increasing the powers of the Council of Ministers to close the democratic deficit. 'Giving yet more power to the Council of Ministers would only exacerbate that problem. It would mark a further shift away from democratic rule toward the rule by "experts" that you so rightly decry.' Two days later Richard Lamming, Director of the Federal Union, wrote urging a strengthening of the Parliament's legislative powers. 'What the people of

Europe are used to is parliamentary democracy where divisions can be on political rather than purely national lines' (*Independent*, 4 and 6 June).

In early July the *Times* claimed that British MEPs were seeking equal pay with other MEPs (11 July) and, some days later, ran a large item on the cost of Parliament buildings and the rivalries between Brussels and Strasbourg over their importance. The newspaper noted that each MEP cost £1 million per year to 'keep in business' (*Times*, 16 July). A week later both the *Telegraph* and *Independent* ran stories on a resolution in Parliament covering the acceptance of gifts by MEPs and the rules governing lobbyists. The *Independent* noted that the resolution had taken seven years to appear while the piece in the *Telegraph* ended by noting that, despite the resolution, MEPs squabbled over the definition of a 'gift' and over the meaning of the lobbyists' code (*Telegraph*, 16 July). The *Times* gave the event more space and ended by quoting Elizabeth Guigou, a French Socialist MEP, to the effect that 'This text is better than the vacuum we have now' (*Times*, 18 July).

The tenor of these pieces on Parliament was clear. As with other EU institutions Parliament seemed to be, from time to time, an expensive nuisance. It did not seem to be important to the British government and electorate but, as time passed, it acquired wider ramifications in the minds of journalists. After the August recess it continued to be a prominent story through September and October. On the eve of the official Parliamentary enquiry into the BSE affair there were publicly vented allegations that the Commission had been involved in a 'cover up' of the dangers present in the meat food chain as early as 1990. A leaked Commission memorandum concluded that the EU veterinary committee had decided in 1990 that 'it was necessary to minimise the BSE affair by using disinformation' (*Financial Times*, 3 September).

Such allegations were widely reported in British newspapers a few days later. Terry Wynn MEP had a letter on the subject in the Independent in which he concluded that the committee was set within a committee structure parts of which met secretly, and that only member governments could make EU 'fully accountable' by forcing more openness (*Independent*, 13 September). The following day the *Financial Times* reported that a Commission official had earlier warned of the imminent collapse of beef prices unless the Commission was given powers to increase stocks promptly (14 September). In London pressures on the government to resist EU demands increased sharply. By 19 September the Cabinet decided not to undertake a selective cull of cattle aimed at eradicating BSE in British herds.

Commission officials were outraged, and on 21 September British newspapers were reporting a Commission determination to continue a total ban on British beef exports. Klaus Haensch, President of the Parliament was quoted as saying 'the UK did not belong to the Union if it abandoned internal solidarity and did not respect decisions' (*Financial Times*, 21 September).

Through October the stand-off continued. Guy Legras, the Commission official who had earlier been accused of organising the 'cover up', admitted that EU monitoring of BSE in the UK after 1990 had been poor because of 'staff shortages'. He denied there had been a cover up but said he wanted to avoid consumer panic 'We are trying to manage uncertainty ... [he said] ... we are in a huge grey area of doubt' (*Financial Times*, 2 October). On 10 October Terry Wynn MEP had a letter in the *Independent* setting the BSE problem in the context of an urgent need for CAP reform (*Independent*, 10 October). On 15 October the Irish Agriculture Minister, Ivan Yates, was reported to be seeking Commission permission to have Northern Ireland cattle excluded from the ban on British cattle since no BSE case had ever been found in Northern Ireland (*Financial Times*, 15 October).

The Parliament's enquiry into the affair continued against the background of a rising awareness of the likely cost to members of BSE eradication. By 28 October the *Financial Times* was forecasting conflict between agriculture ministers faced with plans to cut aid to cereal farmers to meet BSE costs. As November wore on the Parliament buzzed with rumours concerning the outcome of the BSE enquiry. The findings began to be leaked as soon as they were formalised. On 27 November the *Financial Times* reported that the findings 'left few unscathed' in the Commission, the industry or the veterinary profession. British officials stood to be accused of 'inadequate control and poor management' having allowed infected meat and bone meal to be fed to British cattle as late as 1996, eight years after initial restrictions were legislated. The Agriculture Commissioner, Ray McSharry, the Agriculture Commissioner and Guy Legras, were likely to be accused of restricting discussion of BSE in order to protect beef markets. Both were reported to be rejecting all charges arguing that there was an acute shortage of EU inspectors and that, anyway, it was the duty of the UK government to enforce EU regulations. The enquiry found evidence of conflicts between individuals and departments in the Commission. The ban on the export of British gelatine, for example, seemed to have been lifted despite the refusal of a reputable, independent research institute to guarantee its safety, even after special treatment.

Reimar Boge, the chair of the enquiry and a German MEP, spelled out the mix of concerns involved. He was quoted saying that 'the Parliament's reputation rested on the results of the enquiry, the first to be completed under powers given it by the Maastricht Treaty'. He went on to say that 'if we are successful it will prove that the Parliament can use this right of inquiry to find truth and uncover mismanagement'. The Chairman was not unaware that a report which singled out the Commission 'could be used by some member states to argue that the Commission's powers should be curbed'. He was worried, he said, that the report 'should not be misused by politicians' (*Financial Times*, 27 November). Little imagination was needed to guess which industry and which politicians were being pointed to. He knew that British politicians and the beef industry would strongly resist such an assertion of Parliament's influence.

Few stories could match BSE for drama and significance. Parliament, however, had turned to other matters while its BSE enquiry took evidence. British newspapers, especially the broadsheets, averaged some three stories per week throughout the period – no reader could ignore European matters. On 19 September Parliament had voted by 319 to 23 to cut EU aid to Turkey because of its human rights record. The vote cut across earlier willingness to bring Turkey into closer trading relations with Europe though not into membership per se. The *Financial Times* report noted that 'the vote could lead to a dispute with the European Commission and Council of Ministers which believe the aid should be paid' (*Financial Times*, 20 September). On another front a letter from Robin Teverson, Liberal Democratic MEP for Cornwall, attacked EU fishery policy as 'grossly wrong' a sign perhaps that his party was ceasing to be uncritically 'European'. The MEP urged a regionalisation of fishery policy so that historic users in regions could manage fish stocks and outlaw 'quota hopping' (*Financial Times*, 26 September).

Two other items foreshadowed long running stories. A letter from Tony Robinson criticised Rupert Murdoch's BSkyB proposals to monopolise sporting fixture coverage. Interestingly, neither the newspaper nor the author was identified beyond his name though he was in fact an employee of the Socialist Group in Parliament. The *Independent* clearly felt he was voicing majority sentiments in Parliament. Robinson had noted that, following a report from Carol Tongue MEP, Parliament had voted to 'defend public service broadcasters such as the BBC' (*Independent*, 25 September). The issue returned in early November when the *Financial Times* carried letters from Carol Tongue and Sam Chisholm of BSkyB differing sharply on

Murdoch policies. BSkyB, the MEP argued, was out to dominate the digital television revolution by marketing an exclusive decoding box. She noted that 'potential purchasers should be warned that the boxes may soon be worthless as the licence to use them may be withdrawn when ... European law is translated into British legislation' (*Financial Times*, 1 November). This debate involved undertones of protection for the European film industry and 'cultural defence' – both central points of conflict in the previous round of WTO negotiations. Despite its importance, however, Parliament on 12 November refused by 24 votes to insist on 'binding quotas' for European made programmes (*Financial Times*, 13 November).

Looming over all EU news in September, however, was the approaching Dublin Summit. On 7 September the *Independent* had a long article entitled 'Time for Real Euro-democracy' based on a paper by Allen Butt Philip written for the John Stuart Mill Institute in London. The author argued that 'the cutting edge of representative democracy is the making of laws' and, in the EU, the Council of Ministers made the laws. Several national parliaments, he argued, barely scrutinised European legislation and the European Parliament was not strong compared to the Council which met secretly and gave 'member states under-the-counter exemptions or special deals'. The author demanded more Council openness but noted that while 'Democracy is a Euro-cause worth fighting for ... [it is likely] ... to strengthen the EU [despite itself] not weaken it' (*Independent*, 7 September).

Proposals for the Dublin agenda included those for more majority voting, more powers for the European Parliament and more co-decision making in domestic and foreign policy (*Independent*, 5 October). Two weeks earlier large numbers of MEPs in debate had been severely critical of what they saw as a lack of vision and political will by EU political leaders. Among them had been Pauline Green, a London MEP, leader of the European Socialist Party and a long time critic of the British government on European matters. She was well aware that the EMU impetus was flagging in face of the European recession and unemployment. Ms Green said there was 'a mood of disillusion and depression. The Union is dismally uninspiring'. Gijs de Vries, MEP, the leader of the Liberal-Democratic group, argued that 'the credibility of the Union is crumbling away'(*Financial Times*, 19 September).

If the outlook as seen by Parliament was unpromising, events in Austria made the prospect even darker both for MEPs and European political elites. The neo-fascist Freedom Party secured 21 per cent of the vote in the European elections and traumatised sections of the European Socialist Party. As an editorial in the *Financial Times* noted 'with 21 members of the Austrian Parliament, the Freedom Party has gained a voice in Strasbourg and Brussels that will bring comfort to chauvinist movements which are testing the limits of respectability in other European countries' (*Financial Times*, 15 October). Of equal concern to some MEPs was the Helms-Burton resolution in the US Congress which put sanctions on companies trading with Cuba (*Financial Times*, 20 October). Resentment at this 'diktat' continued through November, When the British government decided to support opposition to 'the illegal blockade of Cuba' it found itself thanked in a letter to the *Financial Times* from, inter alia, Stan Newens MEP (*Financial Times*, 18 November). Parliament's opposition to the Helms-Burton resolution had been important in rallying opposition among other European governments similarly. If Parliament for some was still a 'talking shop', it was becoming one which exerted increasing influence.

Other matters of less symbolic significance came before the Parliament at this time. On 1 October it rejected moves to undo a Commission proposal restricting the label 'chocolate' to any substance containing vegetable fat (*Financial Times*, 1 October). Three weeks later Parliament stiffened Commission proposals to control 'cold calling' telephone sales unless they were backed up by 'opt out' possibilities after the sales were completed (*Financial Times*, 24 October).

No subject, however, could eclipse the question of the cost of the European Parliament and especially MEP salaries and expenses. On 30 September the *Daily Mail* attacked MEPs for allegedly being able to pay their pension contributions out of their parliamentary expenses. With approval the newspaper noted that a Dutch MEP had characterised the pension scheme as a scandal and refused to join it. On 25 October the *Independent* reported that Parliament had declared 'austerity' to be the watchword for the coming EU budget and had resolved to retain a portion of the salaries of 20 EU Commissioners until better accounting procedures were established. As it happened, two weeks later – perhaps to the joy of the Commissioners – the expense allowances of MEPs came into question. This followed a British television documentary which alleged that, not only were such expenses too high, but the administration of those expenses was prone to a variety of frauds. Klaus Haensch, the President, rejected claims of widespread fraud and blamed an 'anti-European campaign by the media in one member state' for drawing undue attention to the problem (*Financial Times*, 7 October). As though in a further response the President, the following day, called for equality of salaries between MEPs. The huge disparities between the salaries of MEPs from e.g. Greece and Italy had long been a cause for concern. It was the ground of allegations such as the ones that Greek, Portuguese and Swedish MEPs claimed disproportionate travel allowances. Even worse, it was alleged, expense claims for air and rail tickets or hotel bills did not have to be produced by members when requesting reimbursement. This is no longer true. The television documentary had, somewhat tendentiously, filmed MEPs at Strasbourg claiming the attendance allowance on Fridays just before they left for the airport!

Such allegations were not new but they fed the image of the Parliament as an expensive, powerless 'talking shop' which was a 'gravy train' for members and a scandal for EU generally. Not a few MEPs, however, believed that a Parliament which challenged fraud and maladministration in member countries and the Commission should be a Parliament with clean hands (*Financial Times*, 7 October; *Independent*, 15 October). On 5 November the *Telegraph* itemised the cost of member expenses paid and noted that Poul Schluter MEP was pressing President Haensch to act. A source close to the President was quoted saying 'If Members ... criticise the standards of the Commission and member governments, they cannot go on as they are'. An editorial in the *Daily Express* criticised 'the absurd and remote European Parliament ... [which] ... mainly mirrors the lifeless and impotent debating chambers of most continental nations'. It ended by demanding that those who professed outrage at British political corruption stop finding that 'their rectitude stops at the Straits of Dover' (*Daily Express*, 11 November).

An example of an appropriate response came on 22 November when the *Financial Times* reported a call by a senior Conservative MEP, Edward MacMillan-Scott, for an enquiry into 'serious irregularities' in the accounts of a Commission fund to promote tourism in the EU. This was not a new revelation and the chief administrator, Heinrich von Moltke, had already been arrested by Belgian police. The Parliament, however, resolved that the Commission must lift diplomatic immunity from other culprits in the relevant agency. Once again the Parliament took the chance to assert oversight of Commission activities, one of its prime claims, after all, to power and influence within EU.

Toward Conclusions

This brief analysis of British press coverage reveals the quality of the struggle between newspapers to influence British opinion. The BSE crisis exemplified and heightened British coverage of EU news generally but the tenor of that coverage left some things to be desired. Newspapers concentrated on news and there were few editorials even in pro-EU newspapers like the *Mirror, Guardian, Independent* and *Financial Times*. The hostile press, owned in crucial cases by foreign nationals (Murdoch's *Sun, Times* and *News of the World* and Conrad Black's *Telegraph*), missed no chance to present the downside of EU – bureaucratic, ineffective, wasteful, pretentious and Franco-German in its bias – as these mass circulation papers chose to see it. European Parliament news as such was rare and mostly hostile. What items were not hostile were letters from MEPs which the *Guardian, Financial Times* and *Independent* gave ample room to. Having said that the raw daily news coverage meant that, at least, no reader could miss the fact that it was the Parliamentary inquiry which had publicised the culpability of veterinary experts, the Commission and the European meat industry for its share in the BSE disaster. Equally no discerning reader could miss in the news columns the fact that sources inside EU provided most of the evidence of fraud and mismanagement including expense claims by MEPs. Such a reader would have to conclude that EU institutions did not hide their faults or, eventually, fail to take corrective action. Most British readers in 1996 could not fail to note that in some ways MEPs were no less – and perhaps more – open to criticism than some of their own representatives at Westminster.

6 MEPs, Constituencies, Parties, Mass Media

If I relied on media coverage for satisfaction, I would be suicidal (Conservative MEP, 1997).

Many MPs are myopic on EU, and even Europhiles are deficient in knowledge (Labour MEP, 1997).

Concern in Parliament about its media coverage is not new and, in 1987, was the subject of a study by the Policy Studies Institute of London. It found that Parliament and its members received little or no routine coverage in British national media and, when covered, were covered best by the foreign correspondents of British newspapers or by local radio. The latter's reputation at that time was owed to the BBC having a 'dedicated reporter' in Brussels serving local radio and regional television – an arrangement which did not last. The Report noted that the regional press, being under less news pressure, was more ready to take Parliament and other EU stories.

The Report found that MEPs lacked political weight, were too long-winded and not very professional in their dealings with the media. Conservative MEPs had no role in their party while Labour MEPs, in effect, were expected to defer to MPs and follow the anti-Thatcher line at the expense of any pro-EU views. The Report, finally, concluded that Parliament was seen as relatively powerless, was played down by the British government and was expensive to cover for news organisations. It recommended asking the BBC for more coverage, urged Parliament to use its Information Fund more effectively, and urged MEPs to concentrate on local and regional media. Mass media, it noted, were not interested in publicising Parliament so much as helping frame the British political agenda (Policy Studies Institute, 1987, pp. 27–61).

Little has changed, it would appear. We need now to see what current MEPs think of their media coverage and what reasons they feel explain the coverage they get. Before we do so, however, we need to set MEPs in the party and constituency context which, after all, frames their political lives.

MEPs, Constituencies, Parties

As elected representatives MEPs have to relate to a range of individuals and groups in their parties, constituencies and the wider electorate. Members are conscious that they owe a duty to voters, parties, constituency interests and, to a lesser extent, to organisations which articulate national interests. The constituency electorates they represent are, after all, only parts of the larger electorate which their party either governs or seeks to govern. MEPs are very conscious that they must maintain the support they have and, if possible, acquire new supporters to offset defectors. Currently many Labour MEPs are concerned that, at the next European elections in 1999, they may not have Labour nominations or 'winnable' seats – a party list proportional representation system having been proposed by Mr Blair. Not a few MEPs, additionally, fear they will have to pay for any unpopularity of the then Labour government. Survival, therefore, reinforces duty in their relations with their constituencies and parties.

Fifteen MEPs were asked a variety of questions about these relationships. Respondents were drawn from the two main parties and constitute 17 per cent of the total number of British MEPs. Their responses show a consistency of view but, it has to be admitted, can be no more than suggestive of the outcomes of a larger sample.

Firstly the area of constituency services – the front line of their ongoing local activities. Were constituents generally ready to have their queries and requests dealt with by letter or telephone call or did they insist on meetings with their MEP? The replies indicated that, with exceptions, most individual constituents accepted a letter or telephone call. One MEP summed up for all by noting 'I do not encourage meetings but I never refuse to see a constituent if I can possibly do so'. Almost all members agreed that 'service activities have increased, sometimes sharply'. Only one MEP confessed to not knowing why, while 90 per cent cited a growing awareness of EU and the Parliament in particular. A Labour MEP noted 'many constituents with seemingly insoluble problems feel the answer could be found in Europe'. A Conservative MEP echoed this by pointing to the European Court of Human Rights 'the last resort when they have given up on MPs or the local council'. A Labour member added that '70 per cent of the UK Parliament's work is now on the incorporation of EU regulation' – a fact not widely acknowledged at Westminster and even less in the country.

Office workloads in Brussels and in the constituency office are clearly increasing as EU matters become more relevant to more voters and interests.

When asked how much of this workload was 'dutiful' because the subject matter was not within the Member's competence more than half the respondents estimated about 25 per cent, a not inconsiderable amount. A Labour member spoke for a majority when he said 'I always try to reply even if it only means pointing my constituent in the right direction'. When asked whether MEPs provided dutiful replies to voters who were not likely to be supporters, all respondents replied 'never', one prominent Labour MEP replying stiffly that he had obligations 'to all the voters of my constituency'.

What is clear is that constituency services are forcing MEPs to ensure that both their Brussels and constituency offices are efficiently run. One MEP, for example, said 'I get up to 75 letters a week and 50 of those might involve us in real work to follow up'. Another noted 'we send interim replies when we know follow up will take as much as six weeks'. Good office management becomes critical to progress queries involving many actors in Brussels, London or regional level. This is especially true when each level may encompass actors who do not wish to be seen being unhelpful.

Secondly, questions on Party relationships. Were MEPs expected to be present at constituency and local party meetings? All said they were but since some represented as many as eight Westminster constituencies choices had to be made to maximise time at the weekends. 'I always go particularly to the bimonthly European constituency party meetings', said a Labour MEP. A Conservative member noted wryly that 'local parties do not always wish to see MEPs they regard as having "gone native" on them'. Some MEPs (20 per cent) felt little or no obligation to 'clear' their initiatives with Westminster constituency leaderships but most replies indicated that, as one put it, 'I listen but I make my own decisions'. Some members clearly had problems with their local party leaderships over some constituency issues, but most said this was uncommon. What clearly was not uncommon were occasional tensions between local party leaderships over both EU and national party policies. A Labour MEP referred to problems with 'the recidivist, Scargill wing of my party ... I try to make them see we have no choice, or I tell them they are wrong'. When asked what they saw as the causes of greater awareness and resentment at EU influence a mix of factors was cited by all MEPs. These ranged from 'ignorance', 'misrepresentation of EU in a foreign owned press', through to deeply-held convictions about national sovereignty. A Conservative member asserted that 'across parties there is no mandate for Kohl's integration ... and a strong tradition of independence'. A Labour MEP, in contrast, noted that 'I bring constituency influentials to Brussels when I can so they can see what we do, and why it is necessary – they are usually reassured'.

Several times in 1996, and earlier, MEPs found support from London hard to get. When asked whether national party leaderships were helpful when contacted on some constituency issues members were almost equally divided between those who said yes (47 per cent) and those who felt that the leaderships were not relevant (40 per cent) on such questions. In some contrast when asked whether Whitehall ministries were helpful on constituency matters 90 per cent of members said yes though, as one put it, 'very slow to reply and act.' The rules governing ministries' interaction with MEPs were set out in a letter of the Cabinet Secretary, Sir Robin Butler, and clearly indicated sensitivity over priorities (Robin Butler, 1997) Queries from MPs came first but it was clear that EU matters could not be ignored. Presumably in practice the situation has changed little under a new Labour government.

The question of MEP relationships with MPs over constituency matters must be assumed to be potentially sensitive even when no party line was involved. When asked whether members tried to 'work closely' with MPs on constituency questions the answers were overwhelmingly yes though meetings as such seemed not to be frequent. When asked whether partisanship on such matters made cooperation 'difficult or impossible' most of the replies were guarded though only four members said that collaboration on such matters was 'difficult' while four said it was 'easy'. A Labour MEP noted that 'Our work is not integrated with councillors or MPs – and the latter are suspicious of us'. Most members stressed that much depended on personal relationships, while several noted that, as one put it, 'many MPs are myopic on EU and even Europhiles are deficient on knowledge'. Most replies also noted that collaboration varied by issue and some hinted that intra-party divisions could be as much, or more, of a problem.

If party loyalties or factionalism could be problematic, what of the problems MEPs might have with national organisations which impinge on their constituencies and therefore have to be dealt with? When asked whether such organisations were prompt in replying to queries the answers were mostly yes. Nearly 70 per cent of members felt that such organisations provided adequate information and, where necessary, gave them some access to memberships so that MEPs could explain their party or parliamentary difficulties and opportunities. For the most part this meant publishing a letter in the journal of an organisation or being allowed to address a local or regional branch.

Partisanship, on such matters, could not be wished away – 'trade unions are better than the CBI for us' one Labour member wryly noted. However, 75 per cent of members seemed to feel that partisanship rarely determined responses; more important was, as one Conservative member pointed out, the 'professionalism of the organisation'. Another member added that there had been an increase in interactions between MEPs and hitherto less interested organisations 'since the co-decision procedure was introduced'. A Conservative member noted that organisations 'could be more demanding than they are...even during BSE the tone was always reasonable'. Despite this, however, members remained uncertain whether organisations were increasingly aware of EU and especially the Parliament. One commented that 'if you specialise then interested organisations zero in on you, otherwise they do not'. This was for him no more than a recognition for him that organisational interests determined strategies at local, national and European levels.

At the general level of job satisfaction, replies were clearly positive. When asked whether 'being an MEP ... [had] ... proved to be as satisfying as you hoped' two-thirds of members replied 'yes' or 'more so'. Some, from their comments, had clearly seen being an MEP as a stepping stone to Westminster, or back to it if they had previously been MPs. Most of this group echoed a member who, unprompted, said 'I couldn't go there now since I prefer coalitional to adversarial politics and we are engaged here in much more significant business than is the average MP'. When asked about their principal political problems, most members stressed these were rooted in either ignorance or hostility to EU among Conservatives, or misunderstanding of EU among Labour voters. Some recognised that this state of affairs had been contributed to by the adversarial political tradition in the UK which made 'simple-minded opposition to the other side normal', as one Labour member put it. A minority declared that, so far as they were concerned, advancing their party was their principal political opportunity, though a near equal number of members added that 'advancing the EU cause' was an opportunity they relished.

In all such matters, however, members expressed virtually no satisfaction with the contribution made by media coverage of both Parliament and their own activities. Some distinguished between local or regional coverage and the 'non-existent' national coverage; some found radio journalists more willing to listen and follow up stories than print journalists. One Labour member referred to the 'criminal ignorance' of many London journalists especially at the editorial level. A Conservative member noted that EU news 'is not home or foreign news and is "Westminsterised" when it goes out'. A fellow Conservative replied that 'if I relied on media coverage for satisfaction, I would be suicidal'.

Any conclusions here are premature. A limited survey provides data which can only be suggestive so far as the attitudes of MEPs toward their roles and jobs are concerned. It is clear that they are witnessing a steady rise in lobbying and constituency service activities. Office efficiency in Brussels and in the constituency is crucial both for their EU representative function and their political survival. It is equally clear that tensions over European integration are present in all political parties but the size of the Parliament constituencies means that, to some extent, MEPs are distanced from those tensions unless they wish to exploit them. The proposed change to proportional representation for the 1999 European election may well change this, making many MEPs politically exposed. Any change to the Westminster election system, of course, might alter the political landscape greatly, weakening adversarial and strengthening coalitional behaviour, a development making Westminster possibly more congruent with the European Parliament.

There is a degree of wariness between MPs and MEPs within the same party. This reflects a division of labour but also, among some MPs, resentment at the erosion of their position. Some of this may be reflected, too, in the attitude of ministries – as seen in Sir Robin Butler's letter. The civil service is aware that EU matters are becoming daily more important for them. Until this is publicly acknowledged, however, it is important that civil servants steer clear of being accused of being pro-EU by resentful MPs. No such restrictions limit national organisations in their dealings with MEPs. In pursuit of their interests they target interested or important MEPs and, in some cases, offer opportunities for their personal political gain, but also for EU publicity.

Finally it seems clear that, in an otherwise satisfying job, the largest blot on the MEP landscape is the poor media coverage they and Parliament receive from British media. Most of these members feel that European integration is hampered by the relative invisibility of the Parliament. Members know that it is an increasingly important player within EU and a crucial repository of democratic accountability. Quite why this media invisibility is the case is an important question and one that has now to be examined.

MEPs and Mass Media

The following analysis is derived from questionnaire and interview data from 33 Labour and 10 Conservative MEPs gathered over a period from late 1995 to early 1997. MEPs from all parties are faced with many questionnaires, some masquerading as academic questionnaires. Among Labour MEPs, in consequence, there is a reluctance to give time to surveys except from known investigators or organisations. The field in many ways has been spoiled and I record my gratitude to those members who gave me their time.

The contrast between Labour and Conservative respondents in this sample is quite striking. The all male Conservatives, at 57 on average, are six years older than their Labour counterparts, and 14 years older than the average Labour member in the 1994 intake. Half as many have been councillors in local government and nearly all of them were businessmen or business writers/consultants. Despite the Labour sweep of 1994, 50 per cent of this sample are first-term members, a fact not true for Conservatives overall.

Labour MEPs in this sample show a significantly different profile. Nearly a half have been teachers in schools, colleges or universities and, of those, two-thirds had been councillors. Ten per cent had prior Parliamentary experience as research assistants to MEPs, two had been television researchers, one with the BBC. Only 15 per cent had manual worker backgrounds and of those four had been councillors. While almost all MEPs had trade union sponsorships, only a small minority had worked as officials in trades unions, the Labour Party or Cooperative movement. Officials of interest groups provided two MEPs, one was a minister of religion and another a surveyor. Two-thirds of the 1994 intake were women. Old Left sympathies clearly correlated with the older industrial areas of the country.

The groups then exhibited a clear private vs. public sector division and, given their occupational patterns, a difference of formal education – 13 of the 33 Labour members had postgraduate degrees, three being PhDs (European Parliament, DG III, European Elections 1994).

1 Media Consumption

It is clear that MEPs and their staffs are assiduous monitors of all the newspapers circulating within their constituencies. 63 per cent of members reported seeing up to five newspapers regularly and all claimed to see others 'sometimes'(1). Most members had time to read only one or two newspapers daily and scanned the remainder at weekends. Thus the clips provided by staff were crucial and nearly 90 per cent of members reported a total monitoring of all constituency newspapers by their staff. Limited resources, however, meant there could not be more than intermittent monitoring of local radio or television coverage, though over half of the members claimed this was being done where possible (2). Local radio, particularly, was cited by some members as increasingly important. One member claimed that radio was crucial to his political survival since it allowed him to go around a hostile local press. He believed that it was vital to feed his local radio with stories as often as possible. Most members accepted that political survival required as much visibility as possible in all local media.

At the level of the national press members were less dependent on clips from staff since, in Brussels and Strasbourg, almost all the newspapers they needed were available to them. For Labour MEPs the Socialist Party provided a clipping service for their use. Some 70 per cent of members reported seeing up to five newspapers regularly (3) and a similar number claimed to see some foreign newspapers regularly, the *Wall Street Journal* and *International Herald Tribune* being frequently mentioned (4). One very active member confessed that, given his busy schedule, 'I follow the *European* regularly and anything else drawn to my attention by colleagues'. Parliament, itself, provided a weekly digest of European press coverage and this, while highly selective, was still useful for tips which members could follow up. Clearly MEPs at all levels were assiduous consumers of printed news but were less able to monitor radio and television coverage. British television and radio news could be seen or heard when members are in Brussels and Strasbourg. Except for work pressures, therefore, MEPs need never be out of immediate touch with local and national UK media coverage.

2   Media Coverage Assessed

Consuming media coverage is one thing, finding it palatable is another. In their local press more than half of the members claimed to be dissatisfied both with coverage of themselves and Parliament (5). Conservative MEPs seemed noticeably more dissatisfied than their Labour colleagues. One such member complained of little coverage 'beyond my own press releases'. In contrast another emphasised that while his press releases were mostly ignored, the key constituency newspaper 'takes a column from me'. In relation to local radio some members noted that market pressures made radio, as one put it, 'hungry for more local and European news where it has local reference'.

At the national level, members were clearly highly dissatisfied with the volume and quality of coverage given to MEPs and Parliament – only a minority expressed satisfaction (6). Most of the replies were variants on the theme of 'What coverage'? A long-serving member noted that coverage 'is very nationalistic in all member states ... but very bad in the UK'. One Labour MEP asserted 'I do not attempt a national profile', while another coming from a 'Tory region' noted 'I have news value because of the media need for different angles'. Most members subscribed to the view that EU news is reported, as one put it, 'in a derogatory and dismissive way except in ... the *Financial Times*, *Guardian* and *Independent*'. A Scottish member emphasised that Scottish newspapers – his national papers – were much better.

When questioned on the access provided for journalists few members were unhappy with this at the constituency level (7). At the national level, however, there were doubts – more than half the members questioned whether access was good enough and more will be said on this later (8). When asked whether reporters were willing to use the access provided replies showed a clear pattern. At the constituency level over 70 per cent said 'yes or mostly' with Conservative seeming more negative (9). Nationally some 60 per cent gave clearly negative responses (10). The usual 'health warnings' must apply here. To offer respondents a chance to see distortion in coverage when their own self-interest was involved was an invitation few resisted. To offer it to politicians whose political survival depended on favourable visibility was harder again. To offer it, finally, to members of a legislature who see themselves downplayed in importance was hardest of all. That having been said, the data are enhanced by plausibility and illuminate the working assumption of members.

Answering a question on whether members saw 'distortions' in the presentation of news of Parliament, 56 per cent of the members saw some at constituency level and 85 per cent at national level, with Conservatives again being the most unhappy (11). At the constituency level the principal problem seen by members was the disregard of information they provided (40 per cent of mentions) followed by concentration on some individuals (20 per cent) and the negative quality of news (20 per cent). Journalists, of course, would see these replies as questioning the definition of newsworthiness. Journalists would say that in most democracies the complexity of legislatures and the large number of news sources make it difficult for generalist reporters to write sensible, interesting copy. MEPs, of course, are ready to blame partisanship or incompetence and both must be present to some extent. Only a few members readily acknowledged their own contribution to the situation.

At the level of the national press, perhaps not surprisingly, members saw greater distortions and negative news presentation. More than half saw evidence of a willingness to distort news of Parliament (12). Interestingly their replies suggested that they were not speaking only of their own failure to make national news. One member with long service sadly noted the lack of debate in the national media over 'the amount of democratic powers that have been removed from the elected and transferred to the non-elected'. Virtually all members believed that the Parliament was the key to countering the steady bureaucratisation which they saw happening within EU.

3   MEP Explanations of Media Coverage

Why do these distortions occur, members were asked? The replies at the constituency level covered a range of possibilities with general hostility to EU institutions and policies being noticeably prominent (60 per cent of mentions) and, specifically, publisher/editor attitudes contributing a further 20 per cent of mentions. Interestingly no members cited explicit party politics. At the national media level hostility to EU matters figured prominently (56 per cent of mentions) and publisher/editor bias providing a further 19 per cent of mentions (13). It seems clear that, so far as UK news editors are concerned, a relatively powerless European Parliament does not command front page status. One Labour MEP said scornfully that 'editors are unable to move heads and grey matter on Europe, and are stuck in isolation and a pro-US interest'.

Were British reporters based in Brussels contributors to this relative news famine MPs were asked? Most members found such reporters adequately informed on Parliament (60 per cent of mentions) but too focused on the Commission (52 per cent). A wide gap was seen between broadsheets and tabloids (58 per cent of mentions) and some reporters seemed unable to present news of Parliament in an attractive form (40 per cent) (14). Which of these characteristics determined the choice of story and treatment? MEPs, generally, could not accept the proposition that it was precisely because reporters knew how EU decisions were made that made them unwilling to give front page status to Parliamentary stories. Over 70 per cent of MEPs saw British reporters as partisan in that respect. By covering Parliament as a relatively unimportant part of the decision making process, MEPs felt, the British press helped to keep it so and in this had the tacit support of the Commission and the Council of Ministers.

Had MEPs tried to cultivate London based reporters and editors who, after all, did not work within an EU ambience? While Scots members denied that 'London reporters and editors' were their national press, a senior Labour MEP was quite clear that 'the problem is London, not Brussels'. Not a few members noted that key figures in the London media made little or no effort to get to know MEPs – but 60 per cent of such members admitted they had made no effort themselves to cultivate London journalists. Among those who had done so nearly 40 per cent were happy with the results ascribing the reasons for their success to specialist expertise in one or other policy field (15). As one such member put it 'I have feature editors whom I contact when I want to place a piece' while another added that he had secured 'good results in my field of activity'.

Members were asked whether they saw any differences in the ways British national broadcast media covered EU news. The replies were mostly negative but a minority did voice judgements as between channels. Most Labour members singled out BBC radio news as Europhile while a minority across party lines identified ITN news as Europhobe. Members were more ready to voice technical criticisms of channels. Both Labour and Conservative members characterised broadcast news as 'soundbites only'. Some Conservatives were trenchantly critical of news organisations who were content, as one put it, 'to use MPs as sources on Europe!' Some members characterised regional television and radio as giving more and better coverage than national channels, and added that the local and regional press covered best of all (16). These views are congruent with earlier points made here about the significance of legislative complexity for journalists, particularly those used to the seeming simplicity of the Commons. Journalists focused on breaking news were disadvantaged while those who had more time and space to cover the slower pace of Parliamentary activity seemed to benefit.

4 MEPs – Prescriptions for Better Coverage

What can Parliament expect of British media and what, if anything, can it do to help itself? It is clear that British members feel that they are in a more difficult situation than colleagues from other countries. As they see it such colleagues are the beneficiaries of a relatively tame party press and, in many cases, a pliant EU-friendly public broadcast system. The territorial constituency system poses problems which some members deplore but most feel will not easily be changed. Electoral reform, for example, might be a help but members would still have to cope with long lived national stereotypes on most if not all aspects of EU. Members know that Parliament is routinely portrayed as a 'gravy train' for members and a less than serious check on the 'faceless bureaucrats' of Brussels (17). The current media situation in the UK gives them little hope of a better deal for themselves and Parliament – the commercialisation of the BBC and the 'Murdoch factor' were often cited. Little wonder that when asked whether EU news is better covered in the Union, most members seemed ready to believe it was. 20 per cent of members replying believed that in almost all member countries mass media offered better coverage than did media in the UK – France and Germany being especially singled out (18). It is fair to add that most members stress that this impression was gained, not only from their own limited reading and watching, but also from more knowledgeable opinions held by their European colleagues.

What could Parliament do to improve both its own, and members' interests? The answers covered almost every aspect of Parliament's work and situation – more staff (9 per cent of mentions), more training in media use (9 per cent), more user-friendly documentation (20 per cent), and more background briefings by party leaders (14 per cent). Members, further, felt there should be more coordination of news release between EU institutions and field offices (15 per cent) and far more proactivity in news making by Parliament and its field offices (13 per cent) (19). Most replies, however, gave strong emphasis to the need to acquire television coverage. More user-friendliness by Parliament, members felt, might encourage more television coverage of committee and plenary sessions which, if structured appropriately, might spark greater press coverage and popular engagement.

In fact, during the 1990s Parliament was publishing an ever increasing amount of information on its activities. DG III now has responsibility for two databases – Epistel and Epoque – which provide a huge range of information available to the public and to the staffs of both Parliament and the Commission. Since November 1996 Europarl is on both the internal Parliamentary network and on the Internet. The aim, of course, is to make promptly available all relevant information to members of national, regional and local assemblies, mass media, representatives of socio-political groups, students and researchers. MEPs were already creating Web sites for themselves, a fact of considerable potential significance.

Parliament thus made easily available the documentation of its public debates and decisions plus studies, press releases and details of prospective Parliamentary activities. What, of course, Parliament could not do was to make available material from private, group, and committee discussions which were not meant for publication. Minutes of meetings could be published but, as ever, they might be misleading. DG III was not in a position to dictate simpler procedures, timetable or agendas. The latter was important because, as seen by not a few MEPs, Parliament spent too much time on symbolic matters of a global kind, and not enough time on bread and butter issues they considered relevant to voters. The result was that work which Parliament did was lost in reportage of matters which European voters might regard as marginal at best.

MEPs were fully aware of the above developments and welcomed greater transparency of decision. Asked whether Parliament should take more steps to publicise its achievements very few MEPs disagreed (20). Equally, when asked whether Parliament should generally become 'more user friendly', most members agreed and voiced astringent criticisms of current efforts (21). Members felt that, to secure more radio and television coverage which they saw as crucial, Parliament needed to take command of its expanded information services which should secure more satellite access and be the vehicle for the institution to conduct its own public relations. Parliament, they were certain, could not depend on normal news channels which they saw as too commercialised, partisan, or unduly influenced by national governments (22).

In this members were very similar to their Congressional counterparts in Washington. Facilities to provide for constituency coverage have been expanded to facilitate re-election. In the process, however, distorted institutional coverage harms the image which the legislature would like to project. MEPs would argue that this image problem is not of their making and, in the British case, owes most of its origins to the changing patterns of media ownership and to the partisan battle between the major political parties. In 1996 some MEPs were ready to speculate that the election of a Labour government in 1997 would not make a great deal of difference on EU questions.

Questionnaire for MEPs 1996*

( ) = n
Others = %

1. How many newspapers covering part of your constituency do you read:
   (a) Regularly?
   (b) Sometimes?

	(a) up to 5	5+	n	(b) up to 5	5+	n
Labour	(20) 60.6	(13) 39.4	(33)	(17) 85.0	(3) 15.0	(20)
Conservative	(7) 70.0	(3) 30.0	(10)	(1) 16.7	(5) 83.3	(6)
Combined	(27) 62.7	(16) 37.2	(43)	(18) 69.2	(8) 30.8	(26)

2. Do your constituency staff, or party workers, clip newspaper items of interest to you on a regular basis?
   Do they monitor local radio or television for you?

	Newspapers Yes	No	n	TV/Radio Yes	No	n
Labour	(26) 86.7	(4) 13.3	(30)	(10) 58.5	(7) 41.2	(17)
Conservative	(7) 87.5	(1) 12.5	(8)	(3) 42.8	(4) 57.1	(7)
Combined	(33) 86.8	(5) 13.1	(38)	(13) 54.2	(11) 45.8	(24)

3. What national UK newspapers or magazines do you see?

	up to 5	5+	n
Labour	(22) 78.5	(6) 21.4	(28)
Conservative	(5) 50.0	(5) 50.0	(10)
Combined	(27) 71.0	(11) 28.9	(38)

4 Do you read any non-British newspapers or magazines?

	up to 5	5+	None	n
Labour	(19) 61.2	(1) 3.2	(11) 35.5	(31)
Conservative	(9) 90.0	–	(1) 10.0	(10)
Combined	(28) 68.2	(1) 2.4	(12) 29.3	(41)

5 Generally speaking, are you satisfied with the volume of local media coverage of:
   (a) your activities?

	Yes	No	n
Labour	(12) 54.5	(10) 45.4	22
Conservative	(2) 20.0	(8) 80.0	10
Combined	(14) 43.8	(18) 56.2	32

   (b) news of Parliament in the *local* media in your constituency?

	Labour	Conservative	Combined	n
Very satisfied	(1) 3.0	–	(1) 2.5	2
Satisfied	(13) 43.3	(3) 30.0	(16) 53.3	32
Dissatisfied	(10) 33.3	(5) 50.0	(15) 37.5	30
Very dissatisfied	(6) 20.0	(2) 20.0	(8) 20.0	16
	(30)	(10)	(40)	

6 Generally speaking, are you satisfied with the volume of national media coverage of:
   (a) your activities?

	Yes	No	Mixed	n
Labour	(6) 42.8	(7) 50.0	(1) 7.0	14
Conservative	(2) 22.2	(3) 33.3	(4) 44.4	9
Combined	(8) 34.8	(10) 43.5	(5) 21.7	23

(b) news of Parliament in the *national* media?

	Labour	Conservative	Combined	n
Very satisfied	(1) 3.0	–	(1) 2.4	2
Satisfied	(2) 6.0	(2) 25.0	(4) 9.7	8
Dissatisfied	(22) 66.7	(3) 37.5	(25) 61.0	50
Very dissatisfied	(8) 24.2	(3) 37.5	(11) 26.8	22
	(33)	(8)	(41)	

7 Generally speaking do you think reporters are given enough access to information (news) in your constituency?

	Yes	No	Mostly	n
Labour	(20) 66.7	(6) 20.0	(4) 13.3	30
Conservative	(4) 40.0	(2) 20.0	(4) 40.0	10
Combined	(24) 60.0	(8) 20.0	(8) 20.0	40

8 Generally speaking do you think reporters are given enough access to information (news) nationally?

	Yes	No	Mostly	Don't Know	n
Labour	(14) 46.7	(13) 43.3	(3) 10.0	–	30
Conservative	(4) 44.4	(3) 33.3	(2) 22.2	-	9
Combined	(18) 46.1	(16) 41.0	(5) 12.8	-	39

9 Generally speaking do you think reporters and newspapers are willing to make use of the news facilities open to them?

	Constituency?			
	Yes	No	Mostly	n
Labour	(12) 40.0	(7) 23.3	(11) 36.7	30
Conservative	(3) 33.0	(4) 44.0	(2) 22.0	9
Combined	(15) 38.4	(11) 28.2	(13) 33.3	39

10 Generally speaking do you think reporters and newspapers are willing to make use of the news facilities open to them?

	Yes	No	Nationally Mostly	Sometimes	DK	n
Labour	(3) 10.0	(18) 60.0	(6) 20.0	(1) 3.3	(2) 6.7	30
Conservative	(2) 22.0	(6) 67.0	(1) 11.1	–	–	9
Combined	(5) 12.8	(24) 61.5	(7) 17.9	(1) 2.6	(2) 5.1	39

11 Editorialising apart, do you see any distortions in the presentation of Parliamentary news?

	A little	Constituency A lot	No	n
Labour	(18) 56.2	(5) 15.6	(9) 28.1	32
Conservative	(5) 55.0	(2) 22.0	(2) 22.0	9
Combined	(23) 56.1	(7) 17.1	(11) 26.8	41

	A little	Nationally A lot	No	Sometimes	n
Labour	(4) 13.3	(24) 80.0	(1) 3.3	(1) 3.3	30
Conservative	–	(9) 100.0	–	–	9
Combined	(4) 10.2	(33) 84.6	(1) 2.5	(1) 2.5	39

12 If you do see distortions what forms do they take?

Mentions	Constituency Labour	National Labour	National Conservative	Combined
Overconcentration on some individuals	(6) 23.1	(10) 15.6	(5) 16.0	(15) 15.8
Disregard of news/information	(11) 42.3	(16) 25.0	(8) 26.0	(24) 25.3
Distortion of news provided	(4) 15.4	(22) 34.3	(10) 32.0	(32) 33.7
Only negative news provision	(5) 19.2	(16) 25.0	(8) 26.0	(24) 25.3
Other				
	n=(26)			n=95

MEPs, Constituencies, Parties, Mass Media   65

13 If you do see distortions how to you account for them?
Mentions

Party politics?	Labour		Constituency Conservative		Combined		Labour		National Conservative		Combined	
Hostility to EU institutions?	(10)	27.0	(5)	35.7	(15)	39.2	(14)	7.2	(2)	6.2	(16)	12.3
Hostility to EU policies?	(7)	18.9	(5)	35.7	(12)	23.5	(20)	26.4	(7)	21.8	(27)	20.7
Publisher/editor bias?	(9)	24.3	(1)	7.0	(10)	19.6	(23)	23.5	(7)	21.8	(30)	23.0
Nature of media business	(5)	13.5	(1)	7.0	(6)	11.7	(16)	16.3	(8)	25.0	(24)	18.5
Parliament not 'user friendly'	(6)	16.2	(2)	14.0	(8)	15.7	(17)	17.3	(5)	15.6	(22)	16.7
							(8)	8.1	(3)	9.4	(11)	8.3
	(37)		(14)		(51)		(98)		(32)		(130)	

14 How would your characterise your relations with Brussels based British reporters? Have you found them

A = adequately informed on Parliament?
B = willing to attend party/group briefings?
C = unable to present Parliament news in an attractive form?
D = exhibit a wide tabloid 'v' quality gap in grasp of issues?
E = far too focused on the Commission?
F = partisan in their news coverage?

Mentions	Yes			No			Mostly			Sometimes		
	Lab.	Con.	Comb.	Lab.	Con.	Comb.	Lab.	Con.	Comb.	Lab.	Con.	Comb.
A	(14) 73.7	(5) 26.3	(19)	(1) 50.0	(1) 50.0	(2)	(5) 62.5	(3) 37.5	(8)	(3)100.0	–	(3)
B	(5)100.0	–	(5)	(6) 75.0	(2) 25.0	(8)	(7)100.0	–	(7)	(2) 50.0	(2) 50.0	(4)
C	(3)100.0	–	(3)	(6) 66.7	(3) 33.0	(9)	(8) 88.9	(1) 11.1	(9)	(2)100.0	–	(2)
D	(10) 66.7	(5) 33.3	(15)	(2)100.0	–	(2)	(5) 71.4	(2) 28.6	(7)	(2)100.0	–	(2)
E	(11) 73.3	(4) 26.7	(15)	(5) 83.3	(1) 16.7	(6)	(1) 50.0	(1) 50.0	(2)	(2)100.0	–	(2)
F	(3) 60.0	(2) 40.0	(5)	(2) 66.7	(1) 33.3	(3)	(8) 88.9	(1) 11.1	(9)	(2)100.0	–	(2)
	n = 62			n = 29			n = 42			n = 15		

Combined totals

Mentions	Yes	No	Mostly	Sometimes	n
A	(19) 59.3	(2) 6.2	(8) 25.0	(3) 9.3	32
B	(5) 20.8	(8) 33.3	(7) 29.2	(4) 16.7	24
C	(3) 13.0	(9) 39.1	(9) 39.1	(2) 8.7	23
D	(15) 57.7	(2) 7.7	(7) 26.9	(2) 7.7	26
E	(15) 51.7	(6) 20.6	(6) 20.6	(2) 6.9	29
F	(5) 26.3	(3) 15.8	(9) 47.4	(2) 10.5	19

15 Do you seek to cultivate London based reporters and editors? If so:
(a) yes or no;
(b) with what results?

(a)

	Yes			No		
	Labour	Conservative	Comb.	Labour	Conservative	Comb.
	(13)	(3)	(16)	(18)	(7)	(25)
	81.2	18.7	100%	72.0	28.0	100%

(b)

	Very good	Good	Poor	Very poor
Labour	–	(5) 38.1	(7) 53.8	–
Conservative	–	–	(3) 100.0	–

16 Would you say that there are discernible differences in the ways EU news is presented on:

BBC TV – ?   Europhile
BBC radio – ?   Europhile
ITN – ? Europhobe
Local radio? –
Local television? –
Are there any differences in the treatment of news of Parliament? –

Mentions	Labour		Conservative		Combined	
Sound bites only	(2)	18.1	(3)	27.2	(5)	25.0
Europhile	(6)	54.5	–		(6)	30.0
Europhobe	(1)	9.0	–		(1)	5.0
Use MPs not MEP's on EU	(1)	9.0	(5)	63.6	(6)	30.0
Regional press – better	(1)	9.0	(1)	9.1	(2)	10.0
	n = 11		n = 9		n = 20	

17 Any comment on Parliament and mass media coverage would be welcome

Mentions	Labour	Conservative	Combined
Parliament = 'Gravy train'	(3) 18.7	(2) 40.0	(5) 23.8
UK values	(11) 68.7	(2) 40.0	(13) 61.9
EU fails to explain self	(2) 12.5	(1) 20.0	(3) 14.3
	n = (16)	n = (5)	n = 21

18 Is it your impression that EU news is better reported in other member states? If so, could you give examples?
  – of countries?

	Labour	Conservative	Combined
All	(8) 29.6	–	(8) 20.5
Germany	(5) 18.5	(3) 25.0	(8) 20.5
France	(6) 22.2	(3) 25.0	(9) 23.1
Spain	(1) 3.7	(1) 8.3	(2) 5.1
Ireland	(2) 7.4	(1) 8.3	(3) 7.6
Italy	(2) 7.4	(1) 8.3	(3) 7.6
Belgium	(3) 11.1	(3) 25.0	(6) 15.4
	n = 27	n = 12	n = 39

19 What improvements, if any, would like to see in the ways that Parliament and its members conduct their media relations?

Mentions	Labour	Conservative	Combined
– More staff?	(10) 9.5	(3) 9.6	(13) 9.5
– More training for MEPs?	(11) 10.5	(2) 6.2	(13) 9.5
– More provision of 'user friendly' documentation?	(21) 20.0	(6) 18.7	(27) 19.7
– Regular background briefings by party or party leaderships?	(15) 4.3	(4) 12.5	(19) 13.9
– Greater effort at securing television coverage?	(19) 18.1	(6) 18.7	(25) 18.2
– Greater effort to coordinate news release with Commission and Council of Ministers?	(13) 12.4	(7) 21.9	(20) 14.6
– Expansion of London office activities to pull in national media coverage?	(14) 13.3	(4) 12.5	(18) 13.1
– Other – honest with voters	(2) 1.9	–	(2) 1.4
	(105)	(32)	(137)

20 Do you think that Parliament should seek to use mass media more to publicise its achievements?

Yes	No
(21) 87.5	(3) 12.5

Mention – n = 21 – Yes

More radio/TV	(12)	57.1
Own news agency	(3)	14.3
More EP public relations	(3)	14.3
Own satellite	(3)	14.3

21 In this respect are current party or group efforts to publicise their activities and agendas satisfactory?

Yes	No	Don't know
(2) 6.4	(28) 90.3	(1) 3.2

22 Do you think major EU institutions should become more media conscious and 'user friendly' – and perhaps especially Parliament?

Yes	No
(27) 93.1	(2) 6.9

7 MEPs and Media Coverage – the Belgian and Irish Cases

From the beginning of this study it has been emphasised that the UK's posture toward EU has been relatively unique. A different political history in the twentieth century, differing constitutional norms and conventions, a different electoral system and a differently oriented economy; all have framed different governmental and popular attitudes toward European integration. Media coverage in the UK has articulated these differences. To judge by poll data, to say nothing of the British election result on 1 May 1997, it might well be said that media exaggerated the 'Euroscepticism' of British voters, perhaps for narrow partisan reasons. British opinion on EU seems softer, more ambiguous; in fact more open to a strong lead than conventional wisdom suggests.

Just how different may be demonstrated by looking at two neighbouring countries, Ireland and Belgium, who are perceived as Europhile and staunch proponents of European integration. Is their media coverage of EU and its members very different from that of the UK? Do Irish and Belgian voters regard the Parliament as a vehicle for reducing the democratic deficit and promoting European integration? If they do differ markedly from the UK, to what can these differences be attributed?

As with the UK coverage of EU and EP we examine the Euromedia data for February–November 1996. Based on a wide range of newspapers, magazines and television coverage this offers a broad perspective on the profiles of the two countries – and the EU average figures. We will supplement this data for both countries by a more limited analysis of their press coverage. We begin with the Belgian case.

BELGIUM by John Fitzmaurice, European Commissioner

Table 7.1 profiles Belgian media coverage of a range of issue areas with EU dimensions. As is clear Belgian coverage stays very close to the EU average.

On questions of foreign policy, economics and finance, EU institutions and development, the Belgian figures do not differ from the average in any significant way. Only in the area of competition law do Belgian figures differ sharply from the EU average – perhaps a reflection of having a Belgian, Karel Van Miert as Competition Commissioner. Belgium derives a significant part of its GNP from trade between members. It has an understandable interest in maintaining as great an expansion of that trade as possible – the Commissioner has no trouble securing media coverage. Belgian media coverage thus mirrors the mainstream EU political character of Belgium – passively consensual on EU matters though of late showing a slowly rising tide of concern about some aspects of EU.

Table 7.1 Euromedia – selected issue area coverage – EU, UK, Belgium, July and November 1996

	EU		UK		Belgium	
	July	Nov.	July	Nov.	July	Nov.
Foreign policy	13.1	11.9	9.9	7.2	10.1	14.7
Economic/financial	17.6	27.2	25.1	30.4	18.6	27.2
Industrial affairs	1.2	1.1	0.1	0.0	0.5	0.4
Competition law	6.0	6.0	5.3	3.6	11.6	6.9
Employment/social	6.6	7.5	9.5	18.8	6.7	7.9
Agriculture	10.3	4.9	12.0	4.1	13.8	5.6
EU institutions	8.6	6.1	5.9	6.9	8.9	4.4
EU developments	14.0	15.5	17.8	18.6	9.7	12.3

An analysis of the two leading Belgian newspapers – *La Libre Belgique* (LLB) and *Le Soir* (LS) was undertaken for the month of July 1996 (Liverpool Project). As Table 7.2 shows both newspapers have large newsholes – the space left after removing all advertisements – 89 per cent in the case of the LLB and 80 per cent in that of LS. On average, as Table 7.3 shows, the LLB gave 11 per cent to EU news and the LS just over 3 per cent. The news cover given to Parliament is very small – 0.4 per cent in LLB and 1.2 per cent in the LS. Clearly Parliament is not regarded as, in any sense, comparable to the Commission or Court as a news story.

A further analysis of EP stories was undertaken in order to estimate what these aggregate figures looked like for readers. Over the period, as shown in Table 7.4, the newspapers published 32 stories in the LLB and 34 stories in the LS. On average this amounted to some 2.5 per week in the

Table 7.2 Newsholes – *La Libre Belgique* and *Le Soir*, July 1996

	Average daily total pages	Average daily total ads	Average daily newshole	% of total
LLB	21.6	2.42	19.2	88.60
Le Soir	24.6	4.60	20.2	80.35

Table 7.3 EU/EP news – *La Libre Belgique* and *Le Soir*, July 1996

	General news pages	Political news pages	EU%	EP%
LLB	23.1	24.2	10.56	0.4
Le Soir	26.0	21.9	3.4	1.2

Table 7.4 European Parliament news – *La Libre Belgique* and *Le Soir*, weekly average

	Total articles	Weekly average	MEP focus %	Tendency Neutral/ mild	Tendency Strong view
LLB	32	2.5	80	75	25
Le Soir	34	3.0	80	85	15

LLB and three per week in the LS. Parliament stories thus appeared nearly every other day in both newspapers. What stories were they – what tendency, if any, did they reveal and what was their focus? A coding analysis of this coverage was undertaken. Stories on EP – mentions rather than passing references – were scored from plus three to minus three according to the 'tenor' of their coverage. A score of zero implied neutral reportage; a positive story contained constructive assessments or associated the Parliament or its members with good news; and a minus was given to items which portrayed both as obstructive, irrelevant or corrupt. The analysis suggested that, in both cases, more than 75 per cent of stories were either neutral in tendency or mildly critical or laudatory. Only 25 per cent of LLB stories or 15 per cent of LS stories could be regarded as exhibiting strong opinions for or against the European Parliament and its activities. Eighty per cent of the stories either had an MEP at their centre or mentioned MEPs as part of larger stories on EU policies and their consequences. The BSE crisis received several mentions as did the cost of the new Parliament buildings in Brussels and Strasbourg. The LLB seemed more ready to be critical of EU/EP but only marginally – both newspapers exuded mild disinterest rather than critical engagement. This profile exemplifies the Belgian national posture toward EU which is recognised by Belgians as providing Belgium with considerable net benefits, is seen as inevitable and lacks a competitor for any allegiance in Belgium.

The Political Context

In Belgium, unlike the UK, there has been a long standing passive consensus that European integration is in the long term interests of Belgium. This results from the bitter lessons of her historical experience in the first half of this century. Neutrality and a low profile were not enough to prevent occupation in two world wars. In both cases, this occupation was virtually incidental to Belgium herself, deriving from the strategic needs of her two powerful neighbours, France and Germany. Hence, prevention of conflict between them became an existential matter for Belgium.

Her economy is also among the most open, depending on trade that is dominated by her near neighbours, Germany and France and the Netherlands. Over 50 per cent of her GDP derives from trade. She therefore depends heavily on freer trade and market access. Her history also taught her that for a small state, surrounded by more politically, economically and militarily powerful neighbours, formal sovereignty is of little value. Thus the original premises of European integration – Franco-German reconciliation, integration through opening of markets and permanent pooling of sovereignty – struck an immediate resonance in Belgium. Integration offered a welcome and effective alternative, perhaps the only alternative, for Belgium in the immediate post-war period of evaluation of her national priorities. Thus, Belgium became an early and enthusiastic player, dedicated to making it happen.

After some initial and rather specific opposition from the Socialists to the Coal and Steel Community in the very early years, Belgium settled into a solid pro-European consensus among all the main parties likely to participate in government, including the regionalist parties. Only the now defunct and always marginal Communist Party, and the rightist Vlaams Blok, ever sought to elevate Europe as such into a political issue or sought to offer an alternative vision to that of the prevailing consensus. This is not to say that there has not been criticism of the impact of European policies and the European institutions on certain regions or even localities and economic sectors. These range from the growing sense of distance, alienation, bureaucratic complexity and lack of accountability that is seen by many in Belgium to characterise the EU, through sectoral issues such as prohibition of state aids in favour of ailing industries, to localised concerns such as the environmental impact of growing office space needs of EU institutions, house prices and the impact on the linguistic balance between French and Dutch speakers in the boroughs around Brussels. More recently, the impact on public expenditure and or taxation of the Maastricht criteria has had some political fall out. Europe may not be loved, but equally there is little overt opposition, as the initial grounds for considering integration to be in Belgium's overall and long term interest still hold and outweigh temporary and sectoral negative impact, especially as no credible alternative vision is on offer.

This generally positive, though patchy consensus at elite level is reflected in broader Belgian public opinion, both in terms of observable *vox populi* expression and opinion survey opinion. Broader mass public opinion reflects that consensus more in terms of passive tolerance that has allowed elites to formulate and implement European policy, as they thought fit. Public opinion has never, as for example in Britain, Denmark or Sweden, set limits to the margin for manoeuvre enjoyed by political leaders. More careful examination of Belgian public opinion shows it to be surprisingly complex and ambiguous, if not ambivalent on European issues and indeed much in line with EU-wide trends.

Analysis of recent data on Belgian public opinion towards Europe [Eurobarometer EB 45 (Spring 1996) and EB 46 (Autumn 1996)] show that in the EU as a whole 48 per cent regard membership as a good thing and 17 per cent as a bad thing. For Belgium the figures are 45 per cent good and 15 per cent bad, keeping close to the EU average. Belgium is only very slightly more favourable to integration than Denmark (Denmark 44 per cent). Forty per cent of Belgians consider that Belgium benefited from EU membership and 35 per cent that it had not benefited. This again is close to the EU average. In terms of long-term trends, support for EU membership shows a sharp upward trend until 1990 and then a downward trend to the present figures, representing a position close to that of the early 1980s, before the dynamic period of progress in integration in the mid 1980s. In this the Belgian trend is again close to the EU average. In regional terms (EB 45), the lowest supportive figures are in the areas of industrial decline in

Wallonia (Provinces of Hainaut and Namur) and Vlaams Browband (near Brussels), suggesting that some of the localised issues mentioned above are influencing opinion. Yet, the figures also show that Belgians consider integration too slow not too fast. Fifty-six per cent now support the single currency and only 24 per cent oppose it now well above the EU average in terms of net support. In terms of a positive evaluation of the single market, Belgium had a net positive percentage support level of 17 per cent compared with the EU average of 15 per cent.

Clearly such figures are a mere static photograph and have no absolute value. Nor can they represent an indicator of intensity of opinion or salience. They can though describe trends and suggest tendencies in public opinion. They would seem to indicate some, but not too much dissonance between elite and mass opinion on European issues. They suggest, too, some significant erosion of the more positive indicators of the late 1980s, closely in line with EU averages and EU-wide trends. There is still a soft, passive consensus in favour of European integration, but it has become much less solid than before. Equally though, there is no evidence of significant opposition. Probably, these figures should represent an early warning to the political elite that on European matters, as indeed even more strongly in other areas, public opinion is becoming less passive and compliant. For the moment that does not yet represent any serious limitation on the freedom of manoeuvre of the political elite. Nor is it likely, in the short term, to tempt any significant political force to break out of that consensus to mobilise discontent. The cost benefit of such a step would certainly still be far too negative.

Belgian MEPs in this Context

Where does this general political context leave Belgian MEPs? They must operate within a system characterised by high elite consensus supported by a still relatively intact passive consensus in mass opinion and hence low salience of European political issues. There are therefore few political battles to be won or lost on European issues. At the same time, there is as we have seen some erosion of the passive consensus that previously neither engaged with nor challenged the elite consensus. MEPs must be at the cutting edge of combating that erosion. They may be seen by their party hierarchies as lightning conductors.

The combined effect of the electoral system used for European elections and the political landscape of Belgium creates a situation of stronger intra-party competition than inter-party competition. For the purposes of European elections, the country is divided into two electoral areas which, as it were, overlap in bilingual Brussels. In the north, the Flemish provinces constitute a Dutch-speaking electoral area. The Walloon provinces in the south constitute a second, French-speaking electoral area. Voters in the Dutch-speaking area can only vote for Dutch-speaking candidate lists and voters in the French-speaking area for French-speaking lists. In bilingual Brussels voters can vote for either list. The 25 MEPs allocated to Belgium under the Treaty are then allocated further to the two areas on the basis of their relative weight. Thus 14 members are allocated to the Dutch-speaking electorate and 10 to the French. One is allocated to the German-speaking community in Belgium. This is a purely Belgian matter and is varied from time to time, usually after difficult negotiations. The balance of votes for French- and Dutch-speaking votes in Brussels cannot modify this balance, though it can of course affect the distribution of seats between parties in each of the two electoral areas.

Seats are allocated to the party within each electoral area by applying the D'Hondt divisor method. The political parties present lists of candidates in an order fixed by their own internal party rules, which in most cases for European elections at least give a predominant role to their national executives. Voters may either vote for the list, or express a preference vote for a particular candidate within a list. In theory, it is then possible for preference votes to alter the order of the list and so ensure the election of a candidate placed too low on the list by his or her party to gain election without the assistance of preference votes. In practice this very rarely happens even in national elections, and has never happened in European elections. There are a number of reasons for this despite the tendency for more people to express a preference vote. Most voters vote for the list – preference votes are scattered or are given to well known figures who are already well placed on the list.

In the Dutch-speaking area there have never been less than four parties represented and there are currently six. The same is true for the French. The spread in the number of seats is between one and four. No single party has ever won more than seven seats. Gains and losses at any given election are modest, mostly of the order of one or two seats. Changes in Belgian membership of the European Parliament have therefore been brought about more by political parties than by voters. This means that the re-election prospect of Belgian MEPs depends mainly on mobilising support in party bodies, usually the national executive committees that determine the list and the order of presentation. For parties with a small number of seats or who can be expected to return a smaller number of MEPs at the upcoming election, competition between sitting MEPs for a safe rather than marginal position in a contracting available pool of seats may also be crucial. A complicating extraneous factor may be a strategic decision by a party leadership to head up its list with a key figure not currently in the European Parliament. Two aspects of the Belgian electoral system make this difficult, but it can never be entirely excluded. An MEP may not at the same time be a national MP, a fact that is likely to deter national political figures, whose primary interest is national politics rather than becoming 'working' members of the European Parliament. Secondly, vacancies are not filled by the next non-elected candidate on the main list, but from the 'reserve list', this makes it more difficult for an outgoing MEP to inherit the seat of a leading party figure who resigns shortly after the election.

The 'constituency' that the MEP must seek to influence is therefore small and only indirectly influenced by wider public perceptions of a particular MEP's performance as it may be discerned from the press and media coverage of the MEP's activities or indeed by any objective measure of his or her level of activity. Internal party balance, requirements of providing elected positions to rising party activists, elimination of party rivals from the national political scene, the readiness of the MEP to work for the objectives of the party leadership with the European Parliament as a team player may all be more important than the MEP's record or media profile. Indeed, an independent high profile in the media as an active MEP could, if other factors militate against the MEP in question within his party, be counterproductive for his or her chances of renomination as a candidate. The traditional value of incumbency has therefore to be balanced against other factors. There are clear examples, as with the French-speaking Liberals in 1984, where a party has preferred to put forward a completely new slate of candidates. More often, incumbent MEPs who wanted to seek renomination have been able to do so, though they may not always have been given a free ride, as was indeed the case for one of the most active PSC MEPs Fernand Herman in 1994. This is not to say that personal publicity for individual Belgian MEPs is not sought and is not welcome. It is, however, within the Belgian regional constituency system both more difficult to achieve and less politically valuable to the individual than it is within a single member type system.

Media Coverage and MEPs

Belgian coverage of European issues, as indicated by comparative studies is an average level when compared with other member states. However the nature of that coverage is somewhat different and the possibilities for MEPs to contribute to that coverage are comparatively less than in for example Britain, unless particular Belgian MEPs have some other status, such as M. Deprez who was President of the PSC for 10 years.

Three main European issues can be traced in the Belgian media in the course of the last legislature: economic and monetary union; the BSE crisis; and the role of the European institutions and officials in Belgium. Here, too, the Belgian perspective differs from that in the United Kingdom. There has not been a debate on the merits of economic and monetary union and the single currency that goes with it. There has been little debate on the principle of the convergence criteria and Stability Pact agreed at Dublin that would in effect make these permanent. The debate has concentrated on the capacity of Belgium to comply with these criteria and in particular those relating to the public sector deficit. This debate is essentially a national political debate, dominated by the responsible ministers and party leaders. It is not therefore a debate where MEPs can naturally take the lead.

The BSE debate has been personalised because rarely, a Belgian MEP, Mr Happart (PSE/B) the former Mayor of the Fourons took the lead in attacking the Commission in the European Parliament's Inquiry Committee and tabled a rare motion of censure against the Commission in February 1997. Mr Happart is though the exception which proves the rule. He has a reputation in Belgian politics for raising controversial issues that have brought him into conflict with the political establishment. However, he became isolated in the European Parliament, as he has become in the national debate over the future of the Fourons, a francophone enclave in the Flemish Province of Limburg. He does not act within the Belgian tradition of consensus and compromise and therefore has had little practical impact on Belgian political decision making or European decision-making.

Belgium is the seat of the Commission and other European institutions and some 20,000 European officials and a large number of associated journalists and lobbyists live and work in Brussels. The European institutions have a both positive and negative influence on the Belgian and Brussels economies. The very buildings of the institutions are a major physical presence in the Brussels townscape. A very significant proportion of Belgian media coverage of European issues is concerned with issues relating to the presence of the European institutions in Brussels: cost benefits; asbestos in the Berlaymont; town planning issues; environmental issues; traffic management and congestion; effect on property prices; the salaries and real or imagined privileges of European officials.

More recently, a new conflictual issue has arisen that is peculiarly Belgian. The Maastricht treaty accorded the right to vote in both European and local elections to resident EU citizens. Belgium is not in principle opposed, but regards the issue through the prism of her own community politics. In Brussels institutions, there are reserved rights for the Flemish minority in the bilingual Capital Region, based on a minimum percentage critical mass of voters for the Flemish political parties in the capital. In the immediate outskirts of the capital, in the boroughs that are officially in the Flemish language area, there are often French-speaking majorities or near majorities due to the shift of population from the city centre. The balance is often close from one election to the other. It is assumed that the Flemish parties will receive little support from EU residents either in Brussels or the surrounding boroughs, reducing their political representation and their political weight. This is clearly a national and even a localised issue. The media will not seek out the views of MEPs on these issues. The running will be made by regional parliamentarians, local councillors and spokespersons for political parties and organisations on the ground in the affected areas.

More generally, the very large press corps present in Brussels can have easy direct access to Belgian government, EU institutions, and local players. Lines of communication are flatter and thus there is less need for the mediating and educative role of MEPs in Belgium.

IRELAND by Professor A.C. Collins, University College Cork, Republic of Ireland

European Union News in Irish Media – An Overview

The European Union receives a very high level of public approval in the Republic of Ireland. This favourable outlook is augmented by Ireland's status as a substantial net beneficiary within the EU financial system. Nevertheless, the attention paid to the European Parliament is scant compared to the coverage of the Commission or Dail Eireann, the Irish Parliament. The European Parliament has only 15 members from the Republic and elections to it are 'second order' business. The Irish public is well disposed to the Parliament but does not regard it as very important. Turnout at the last EP election in 1994 was just under 44 per cent, a new low for Ireland.

Context

Unlike many other countries which have become independent in the twentieth century, the Republic of Ireland has remained a stable liberal democracy with fair and competitive elections, alternating parties in government, an independent judiciary and unchallenged civilian control of the military. It also enjoys a vigorous and variegated free press, and broadcasting services of high journalistic as well as technical standards.

The press in Ireland certainly seeks to have an influence on the politics of the nation. Until the 1930s, there were just two main national daily papers. The *Irish Times*, the voice of Irish Unionism before independence became, and remains, non-party. Ireland's daily 'paper of record', it arguably produces both the most serious and the most radical journalism in the Republic. It is run by a trust and has a specific brief to advance the cause of a pluralist and more liberal Ireland. The *Irish Independent*, and its evening and Sunday sisters, are also at the quality end of the market by international standards; supporters of Cumann na nGaedheal during the early years of independence, they are now less uncritical in their backing of its successor Fine Gael and frequently espouse 'new right' thinking, especially on the economy.

The lack of a newspaper supporting Fianna Fail led deValera to set up the *Irish Press* soon after his party first came to power in the 1930s. It quickly became the most popular paper in Ireland and led the market for nearly 50 years. However, in the 1980s the *Irish Press* and its evening and Sunday stablemates not only became less closely identified with Fianna Fail (despite remaining in the hands of the deValera family), but also fell on hard times. The group was the subject of several rescue attempts but finally expired in 1995 – occasioning considerable shock and dismay even among its rivals.

The morning national press now consists of four main newspapers: the two remaining traditional dailies; the *Daily Star*, a less sensational version of the British newspaper of the same name (jointly owned by the British *Express* and the *Irish Independent* groups); and the successful non-aligned provincial newspaper, the *Cork Examiner*, relaunched as the *Examiner* in the hope of picking up at least some of the former *Irish Press* readership.

Sunday offers a wider choice, including a colourful tabloid specialising in scandal and a specialist business broadsheet. A newspaper first published in 1996 devoted entirely to sport is now a general Sunday broadsheet. There is also a lively, and often political weekly provincial press in Ireland, meshing neatly with the concern of so many politicians with parish pump issues. At the same time, there are considerable worries about the penetration into Ireland of British newspapers – the tabloids in particular – which sometimes cost less than half the price of their Irish counterparts.

Irish newspapers are notable for their restraint in reporting on the personal lives of people in the public eye, especially politicians. But like the free press everywhere they have frequently been the progenitors of major policy change especially as a consequence of good investigative journalism. The same has been true of Irish radio and television. Radio Telefis Eireann (RTE) is the state broadcasting organisation; it is responsible for two television and three main radio channels, and has recently been joined by a mushrooming independent radio sector. Despite the fact that RTE (like the BBC in Britain and public broadcast stations in the USA) is legally required to be politically non-partisan, it has been a significant force for social and it follows political change. There is a perception, at the same time, that RTE has lost its cutting edge. Major stories of Irish political interest – such as that which led to the setting up of the tribunal on possible abuses in the beef industry – have been broken on British television which is available almost everywhere in Ireland. This has given added impetus to the drive to set up a third, independent national television network. Also opened in 1996 was Telefis na Gaeilge, an Irish language station.

It is notoriously difficult to measure the influence of the press, radio and television on public opinion, still more to gauge the effect which they have in convincing politicians that change is necessary in this or that area of public life. It is none the less impossible to deny that free and independent media are crucial components of a modern democracy. In this respect, Ireland is well served.

Study Period

The research for this report included a review of the newspaper coverage of the EP during May, June and July 1996. Additionally, in a series of semi-structured interviews with MEPs from each of the major parties questions were asked about press, television and radio coverage of the EP. MEPs outlined their own efforts to attract public attention as part of their work.

Contacts were also made with members of the Irish media, civil service and European movement. The EP office in Dublin was particularly helpful in providing meeting rooms, press archives and contact names and addresses.

No period of three months can be regarded as 'typical.' May to July 1996, however, did serve to highlight the difficulties which MEPs experience in relation to the national media. In March, the Fine Gael/Labour government had published its White Paper on foreign affairs. This had stimulated an unusual level of debate about Irish foreign policy in which the European Union was regularly described as having a 'pivotal' role. Nevertheless the press coverage mentioned the views of European Parliamentarians only tangentially. At the level of 'high politics' government ministers have their views reported but their focus is on the Council, the Commission and the Presidency. All the parties represented in the Dail favour the European project so the debate in Ireland takes place within an overarching consensus. The left-right spectrum is also narrow so none of the policy issues which arose in the study period involved a radical questioning of European policy. Apart from the Greens and Independent, all the MEPs are in parties which have recently served in coalition governments and this further reduces the intensity of partisan exchanges.

If we look at Irish data from the same Euromedia source the impact of the Irish Presidency and the Dublin Summit is clear. Table 7.5 shows that on areas such as foreign policy, economics and finance, EU institutions and development, and the Social Chapter Irish totals either exceed the EU average or come very near to it. The centrality of EU-related news areas could not be clearer. The BSE crisis at first was not a crisis for Ireland except in its role as the holder of the Presidency. As time passed, however, the Ulster angle became a matter in which the Republic had an interest and media reflected this. The potential damage to the Irish meat industry galvanised Irish politicians, especially when they saw xenophobic and anti-EU elements in the British official position. The passive consensus on EU visible in Ireland, as in Belgium, began to fray at the edges.

At the national press level Table 7.6 shows the size of the newshole which, as in Belgium, is high – varying between 81 and 90 per cent. Table 7.7 presents data on the breakdown of that newshole. Strictly 'news' items consume some 85–96 per cent of the three dailies and 62–70 per cent of the two Sundays. Within that total political news takes between 20 and 30 per cent, and of that total EU news items takes between 16 and 22 per cent of the dailies and 15–18 per cent of the Sundays. News of Parliament is minuscule in aggregate taking between 0.4 per cent and 2.8 per cent of

Table 7.5   Euromedia – selected issue area coverage – EU, UK and Ireland, July and November 1996

	EU		UK		Ireland	
	July	Nov.	July	Nov.	July	Nov.
Foreign policy	13.1	11.9	9.9	7.2	15.7	15.4
Economic/financial	17.6	27.2	25.1	30.4	16.0	20.9
Industrial affairs	1.2	1.1	0.1	0.0	2.2	2.0
Competition law	6.0	6.0	5.3	3.6	1.3	2.0
Employment/social	6.6	7.5	9.5	18.8	9.9	8.5
Agriculture	10.3	4.9	12.0	4.1	6.1	4.9
EU institutions	8.6	6.1	5.9	6.9	15.7	10.9
EU developments	14.0	15.5	17.8	18.6	11.5	11.7

Table 7.6   Newsholes – Irish national newspapers, May–July 1996

	Average daily total pages	Average daily total ads	Average daily newshole	% of total
Irish Times	32.3	30.4	28.9	89.5
Irish Independent	32.2	3.2	29.0	90.0
Examiner	29.6	2.1	27.6	93.2
Sunday Business Post	23.6	4.1	19.5	82.6
Sunday Tribune	30.0	5.5	24.5	81.6

Table 7.7   EU/EP news – Irish national newspapers, May–July 1996

	General news pages	Political news pages	EU%	EP%
Irish Times	96.2	29.8	22.0	2.8
Irish Independent	84.8	24.8	15.7	0.4
Examiner	99.3	25.5	19.2	2.3
Sunday Business Post	69.8	21.0	15.2	2.8
Sunday Tribune	62.0	30.0	18.0	0.66

political news items. The conclusion is clear – EU news items are a significant proportion of Irish political news coverage but Parliament items are a small proportion.

Turning to a distribution of EP items as shown in Table 7.8, it is clear that newspapers differ significantly. The Sunday newspapers have as little as one item per month. The dailies, however, are more generous with their space ranging from the *Independent* (one per week), the *Examiner* (two per week) and the *Times* providing one every other day on average. The national newspapers, however, commented editorially and in features on the significance for Ireland of the six month period of EU leadership. The EP was afforded only very brief mentions in all but one leading article. The exception was in the *Sunday Tribune* which linked the role of EP to the broader questions of European enlargement and integration which had to be resolved (*Sunday Tribune*, 23 June 1996). As in Belgium, so in Ireland the focus of these news items is clear. EU news is overwhelmingly focused on MEPs and their activities – 90 per cent in the *Independent*, 85 per cent in the *Examiner* and 75 per cent in the *Times*. Only the latter gives any regular space to the Parliament as an institution operating independently of Irish MEPs.

Table 7.8 European Parliament news – Irish national newspapers, May–July 1996

	No. of mentions	EP/MEP story
Irish Times	42	28
Irish Independent	13	11
Examiner	24	17
Sunday Business Post	3	0
Sunday Tribune	4	2

An examination of the seven provincial papers as shown in Table 7.9 turned up 57 items on Parliament or its members in three months. Of these four (7 per cent) covered the Parliament as such while 53 (93 per cent) concentrated on a local MEP angle or EU news in general. While the latter was big news it either appeared as the activities or utterances of MEPs or a Dublin government response to happenings in the Commission or Council. On both national and local level therefore the pattern is clear. Political news consumes on average 25 per cent of total news and EU news about 20 per cent of political news – the bulk of that being focused on Dublin ministers,

Table 7.9 EU/MEP news – Irish provincial press, May–July 1996

	No. of stories	EP %	MEP %
MC LP DD LE WNS OT CN TT LL SC CEE WMT	57	7	53

MC – *Meath Chronicle*, LP – *Limerick Post*, DD – *Donegal Democrat*,
LE – *Leinster Express*, WNS – *Waterford News and Star*, OT – *Offaly Topic*,
CN – *Carlow Nationalist*, TT – *Tullamore Tribune*, LL – *Limerick Leader*,
SC – *Sligo Champion*, CEE – *Cork Evening Echo*, WMT – *West Meath Topic*

TDs or MEPs. Parliament is not seen as a big EU player but Irish MEPs and ministers are.

A coding analysis of Irish news was undertaken following similar criteria to those for Belgian news – the data is presented in Table 7.10. All the daily newspapers, according to this simple and subjective method, are overwhelmingly positive about the institution. As in Belgium the news items reflected the passive consensus on EU, being mostly neutral or supportive. Comparing the Sunday newspapers, the *Sunday Business Post* seemed more critical than the *Tribune*. Among the dailies the *Independent* and *Examiner* were more critical than the *Times* in which criticism was rare.

Table 7.10 European Parliament news – Irish national newspapers, May–July 1996

	Tendencies for/against Neutral/mild	Tendencies for/against Strong view
Irish Times	96.4%	3.6%
Irish Independent	100.0%	0.0%
Examiner	94.0%	6.0%
Sunday Business Post	100.0%	0.0%
Sunday Tribune	75.0%	25.0%

All three dailies, however, generally provided supportive coverage. As with the Belgian case the contrast with the UK was striking.

Irish television coverage of EP over the same period was analysed and the data is given in Table 7.11. News of EU/EP was not frequent but, it should be remembered, British television news broadcasts are available and

Table 7.11 Irish Television (RTE) – EP coverage, May–July 1996

1	7 May 1996	–	EU funding for Ireland.
2	16 May 1996	–	Maternity leave for MEPs.
3	21 May 1996	–	Debate on soccer hooliganism.
4	22 May 1996	–	Agricultural policy and BSE.
5	22 May 1996	–	British warning to EU on BSE.
6	25 May 1996	–	The week in politics. Soccer hooliganism.
7	1 July 1996	–	Europe debate: who runs Europe?
8	16 July 1996	–	Irish beef industry – special needs.

widely watched. On the state television service over the period there were seven news stories focused on Parliament, the longest being on EU moves to curb soccer hooliganism. Additionally there was a major hour-long item 'Who Runs Europe?' which focused on the potential and limits of Irish influence.

Irish MEPs secure local press coverage easily and national press coverage relatively frequently. In this they provide a real contrast with British MEPs though not with their counterparts in Belgium. The Presidency probably exaggerated coverage of all EU news and we now need to set this aggregate data in the full context of the Irish political and media situation.

Range of Media Coverage

Despite the Presidency and the associated coverage by RTE and the *Tribune*, the range of media coverage was narrow. For the most part, even at a time of heightened awareness of Europe, the media coverage of MEPs was distinctly 'low politics'. In particular, parliamentarians were most often featured in brief, inside page stories about relatively minor issues. Some stories did relate to important topical matters such as duty free shopping, the management of fish stocks and soccer hooliganism. The MEPs' comments were, however, seldom reported in the context of EU decision-making. Television coverage matched that of the newspapers with a similar concentration on topics such as football hooligans though one two minute item did use footage from an EP committee meeting. Television also gave prominence to the difficulties of MEPs securing maternity leave, a fact highlighted by Patricia McKenna MEP during her pregnancy.

The aggregate data, shows a familiar pattern. Relative to the EU as a whole, Irish press interest was higher for agriculture, employment and regional policies but lower for competition and environmental areas. On the whole Irish media did not show any marked difference from its foreign counterparts – economic and financial news provided the staple content. Analysis of coverage of the EP in the provincial papers shows an even more marked emphasis on local issues. There was a propensity to concentrate on the financial benefits of EU membership and the role of the local MEP in directing these to their constituents. Seven provincial papers were surveyed for the three months of the study. Each article mentioning an MEP or the EP was assessed in terms of content, length, tone and position in the newspaper. Generally, stories were fairly positive but brief and seldom in a prominent place. Few were accompanied by a photograph though one exception in the *Leinster Express* had six. This latter piece was one of several which followed visits to the Parliament by local journalists. By-lines were not always given, but where they were indicated they were clearly the work of a freelance journalist who specialised in European affairs and the tone was positive.

Criticisms of government ministers, for example, for failing to defend Irish farmers' interests strongly enough followed party lines. Criticism was usually reported as a small part of the general story. Interestingly, on occasions when Irish MEPs were united in criticising EU policy, the national media coverage was more prominent and positive. Thus, for example, when the Commission proposed cuts in the European fishing fleet only Green MEPs expressed support while others were reported for their opposition. Similarly, BSE related stories often found MEPs in near unison. On all major EU stories, however, coverage of ministers far outweighed that of MEPs.

Given the tendency for major issues to be 'captured' by others, MEPs have sought to establish a public profile. Mary Banotti, for example, has used her long association with family issues to good effect. In the study period she received broad publicity in the national press for a report on child abduction. She called on the President of the Council of Justice Ministers for action: under the Irish Presidency the President was none other than her sister Nora Owen. To an extent, once an issue is raised to prominence by an MEP, it is inevitable that rival politicians, especially ministers, will compete to use it for publicity. In the case of child abduction, the Irish Government did take up the topic during its Presidency.

The Process of Media Coverage

Coverage by the media of EP sessions has been facilitated by monthly visits to Strasbourg by Irish journalists. The EP office in Dublin supports these trips financially. The Irish group includes reporters from the *Irish Times*, RTE, freelance reporters for regional newspapers and radio and a staff member, often the editor, from a regional paper. Freelancers have established markets for syndicated material but their work is chiefly viable because it has attracted subsidies from both the EP office in Dublin and the Department of the Taoiseach. The *Examiner*'s Brussels-based reporter sometimes joins the EP-funded group. Interviews suggested that such trips were useful but reporters needed more than one to learn the *modus operandi* of the Parliament. Such views were seen by some editors as well based but, equally, gave them a chance to allow a hard working journalist a break from the regular routine. The time difference between Dublin and Strasbourg was cited as an advantage for filing stories. The Parliament has changed its arrangements for voting in recent years in a way which facilitates Irish journalists sending items to their news desks in time.

The non-Dublin sources of news on the EU are dominated by Brussels-based correspondents of RTE, the *Irish Times* and the *Irish Independent*. Each of these is primarily accredited to the Commission from which most stories originate. Such reporters have to cover Belgium and other continental news. Paedophiles and their victims dominated news from Belgium during the study period and tended to blanket other EU stories. Mary Banotti received coverage of her suggestion that paedophiles should be electronically tagged to enable monitoring by all European police. This story was based on her speech to the World Congress Against the Commercial Exploitation of Children in Stockholm which was covered in August by Dublin-based journalists. The coverage, however, did note that Ms Banotti was the Mediator on Abducted Children for the European Parliament.

Responsibility in the Parliament does give a member some publicity advantages. Thus, as an example from the study period, Gerry Collins was reported saying that a strong case could still be made for continuing EU structural support into the next century and called for the establishment of regional structures. This item received publicity because he was presenting a report on Ireland's use of structural funding to the European Parliament's Regional Affairs Committee.

The process of reporting is influenced by the arrangements that the party groups adopt for handling press releases from the Parliament. Large groups, particularly the Socialists, offer more support in terms of specialist personnel but also impose disciplines on what can be released to the press and by whom. The aim of most parties is to ensure that on any issue there is no more than one member taking the lead in each member state. Clearly in smaller or technical groups this is less of an issue. When an MEP is the only Group member in the Republic, he or she is at an advantage in terms of resources and media exposure. This benefit extends to being able to buy advertising space to publicise party meetings, seminars and constituency 'clinics'. Irish MEPs are in five of the six biggest groups. Only one, however, is in the largest, the Socialists, and half belong to the rather peripheral European Democratic Alliance.

The Irish media report the EP using local party labels almost exclusively. Thus, MEPs are seen as national parliamentarians at one remove. Journalists take the view that Irish readers would not recognise the official names of EP party groups. Occasionally, however, the full titles are introduced in longer news items. Nevertheless, six of the 15 members from the Republic have never been TDs and two more are now better known as MEPs rather than former deputies in the Dail.

Media coverage of the EP in the Republic includes sources in both Britain and Northern Ireland. Most obviously, the UK television, radio and newspapers that are available throughout the island cover the EP to some degree. The manner of such coverage is frequently negative. British newspapers do, however, sometimes quote Irish MEPs on stories which are not covered by the local media. An address by the Irish foreign minister, Dick Spring, to the EP during the study period, for example, was given quite a different 'spin' in British newspapers. Irish papers sometimes reflect the generally hostile tone of the British press by using the news services offered by the *Times* (London) and others. The *Irish Independent* is the most frequent user of British news services for stories about the EP. This trend seems to have increased since the study has ended.

The monthly journey to Strasbourg is often seen as a bothersome interruption to a Brussels-based journalist's professional and domestic arrangements. Four days on generous expenses but, they feel, with little prospect of a story. News editors in Dublin are reluctant to query what such journalists file and, for this reason, Brussels-based journalists are key gatekeepers for EU news in Ireland. When Dublin-based journalists visit Brussels their stories usually cover a Council of Ministers meeting or focus on better known actors such as the Commission President or the Irish Commissioner. The specialist farming press in Ireland, notably the *Farmers' Journal*, provides regular and detailed coverage of European affairs. The coverage centres on the Common Agricultural Policy an area in which EP has little influence. The Parliament is thus presented as generally hostile to farmers' interests but thankfully an almost powerless enemy.

Parliament still rarely finalises a decision since that privilege lies with either the Commission or the Council of Ministers. Further Parliament usually votes on Thursdays so, for journalists, there is little of the tension associated with votes in the Irish Parliament. Only very occasionally does questioning of Commissioners by MEPs produce 'good copy'. While the influence of British and Irish members has enlivened such questioning there is, however, no real equivalent to the 'political theatre' which exists in the Dail or the House of Commons. For journalists debates in the EP do not lend themselves to easy coverage. As one put it 'there is a big difference between covering Parliament and covering MEPs. They are personalities in their own right and interesting as such'. The inference for Parliament is clear.

Cork and Dublin MEPs target evening newspapers as well as the dailies. Unfortunately this project could not analyse the evening papers systematically. Impressionistically they do not differ much from the dailies – for all of them many stories do not come from Brussels, Strasbourg or Luxembourg but are filed locally.

A perennial problem for the EP is the widespread perception that its members are rewarded too generously with salaries, expenses and other perks. This perspective has outlived various changes the Parliament has made to its accounting system. The most negative story in the non-Dublin press during the study period was headed 'Fat cat MEP pay scandal' (*Cork Examiner*, 27 May 1996).

The Irish voting system, political culture and narrow ideological spectrum results in a high level of personality-based electoral competition. It is, therefore, important to distinguish between media reporting of Parliament and the coverage given to individual MEPs. Politicians, naturally, are most concerned with their own profile in their constituencies. A story with a positive spin in the local newspaper may be more highly valued than an analysis of the place of the EP in the constellation of European institutions. The provincial press reports Parliament, if at all, mostly by reproducing syndicated material which presents it in a positive light. MEPs, like TDs, are mostly responsible for their own local publicity and the provincial press provides a relatively neutral conduit for their publicity efforts.

The national media are more proactive and, generally, are just as well disposed to the Parliament. The majority of material used comes from press releases and speeches of Irish MEPs. The EP rarely makes the front page, photographs seldom accompany stories but the tone is generally favourable. The *Irish Times* is by far the most likely location for any EU story while the Irish Independent is both more critical and less interested. Television coverage of both MEPs and Parliament is intermittent. Indeed, as observed earlier, this study may have exaggerated the attention given to the EP because of the extra programming resulting from the Irish Presidency.

The European Parliament and its members are growingly important within EU. The Parliament's importance is already such that lobbyists and other sophisticated observers of political power are increasingly attentive to it. Public perceptions in Ireland lag behind this assessment and, generally, Irish media do not correct public perceptions. In this, as we have seen, they are little different from their Belgian and British counterparts. In fairness, however, it is necessary to add that, since the study period, the *Irish Times* now produces a monthly report on the European Parliament.

Conclusion

Both Ireland and Belgium exhibit historical differences in their constitutional and media situations. Both, currently, are successful small country players within EU. Each exhibits, as has been shown, a supportive passive consensus on the Union and its evolution. Ireland has disproportionately benefited from the CAP and other EU funds, has acquired a larger international persona and profile within EU as it has freed itself from the shadow of its large neighbour, the UK. Belgium, too, has benefited greatly from the Union in terms of trade and jobs but, as important, has built an identity as the seat of EU's 'capital' and a significant EU player, an identity which helps counter well documented 'pillarising' trends in almost all areas of Belgian life. Of both countries it could be said that if EU did not exist, they would have to invent it.

Mass media coverage in both countries reflects these realities. EU news has been nationalised and is rarely the source of political conflict – EU is the framework within which national politics and discourse are now conducted. By contrast EU news in the UK in 1996 reflected real elite and mass dissensus which was held to frame the coming election – correctly as it proved. Thus in Ireland and Belgium EU news was reported as news about an old established, ongoing process whereas EU news in the UK reflected a real cleavage not only over further integration but over EU membership itself. In the event, of course, the 1997 result seemed not to justify the degree of media emphasis on dissensus. The collapse of the Conservative position and vote meant that such dissensus appeared as a minority party phenomenon. It could not be said, however, that the anti-Conservative Commons majority, or popular vote, was wholly consensual on the question of further integration and the Labour government's policy thus far reflects doubts on that process.

All of which suggests that national political situations, and not structures, are the key determinants in the volume and distribution of all aspects of EU news. The usual explanations of news profiles – the nature of the news business (the rise of television, media ownership), the openness of EU sources (secretive Council and Commission, open but weak Parliament) or local electoral systems (UK vs PR systems) or patterns of partisanship (passive consensus vs active dissensus) appear to be influential only in so far as they help frame elite and mass perceptions of the national situation.

Such a conclusion reinforces the commonsensical view that 'news' is information which fits a country's interests, however self-defined. Such interests are articulated by governments and political leaderships but are not created by them and cannot be ignored by them, by journalists or media 'moguls' of whatever kind. Belgian and Irish profiles, further, are suggestive of what can be expected by way of EU news where a generally supportive consensus is present. Belgian and Irish coverage is average EU coverage because such a consensus does exist. The Parliament inside that average news profile is no more the beneficiary of such a consensus than it is in the UK. Parliament is not seen, for example, to be the best hope of reducing the 'democratic deficit' – a conclusion that differs little from assessments expressed in the UK media.

This is the context of Parliament's coverage. Its institutional coverage in Belgium and Ireland is not large because both countries are happy with EU as it evolves. Parliament's coverage in the UK is not large because the level of latent dissensus on the EU and its evolution makes the Parliament a minority question. The Parliament is not seen as a way of making EU more acceptable and hence it is not worth too much attention. However in all three countries MEPs are able to secure higher local profiles than the institutional problems of coverage suggest. MEPs regularly make news but the Parliament as an institution does not.

8 Conclusions and Epilogue

The data for this study was gathered over a period extending from spring 1995 to spring 1997. All data-gathering had ceased before the Labour Party won a sweeping election victory in May 1997. It is, as yet, too early to assess the full effects of that victory on media coverage of the EU and EP.

This data makes clear, firstly, that aggregate UK media coverage of EU matters differs little from that of most member countries. When differences are visible these reflect either government policy or popular concerns – single currency, foreign policy, BSE, fishery policy and so on. All member countries exhibit somewhat similar particularities within their aggregate totals. British coverage, to be sure, is probably more critical of EU matters than is coverage in some countries but the difference is less than popularly imagined, and minimal in the news as opposed to opinion columns. Seasoned observers of media coverage in Brussels are well aware that the appearance of hostility in British coverage is, firstly a part product of British non-coalitional, adversarial political styles and, secondly, the fact that the UK has 'nationalised' EU problems, treating them as part of its ongoing 'normal' political debate. Such observers are likely to add that, despite much lip service to the 'European idea' in for example Spain and Italy, their electorates have yet to be engaged by the finer details and consequences of full integration (Morgan, 1995).

The data, secondly, make clear that British media coverage, though increasing on EU matters in general, still focuses on the Commission and Council of Ministers even though the Parliament has acquired growing importance in EU decision-making. National media coverage of the Parliament is sparse, sometimes hostile, and, too often, in the 'gravy train mode' which fails to recognise this change. In local media, conversely, MEPs secure increasing coverage in columns, letters and pictures in the press, and are finding local radio and television increasingly accessible and useful. The European dimension is visible and significant in local media which, generally, give it the credit and respect it deserves. Labour MEPs in 1996 began to coordinate their press releases and publicity to a degree never before attempted. With a Labour government in power they may also be able to stress their national access to policy making as never before. Concerned, as many are over their 1999 re-election prospects, this angle has already become important as 'Old' and 'New' Labour adjust to each other. Current arguments over systems of proportional representation symbolise and reflect deeper ideological concerns (*The Times*, 22 October 1997, p. 10).

The data, thirdly, suggest that differences in political culture and electoral systems appear to have few consequences for the nature and volume of coverage. Both in Belgium and Ireland coverage is MEP focused to a large extent though this, in contrast to the UK, has more of a party than a territorial reference. In all three countries Parliament as institution is not treated as a major actor so far as democratic accountability is concerned.

The data, fourthly, suggest that the Parliament has a major communication problem. It has the problems of a deliberative assembly – delegation, complex procedures, slow decision making – which at best can make it only intermittently newsworthy. But Parliament has to contend with eleven official languages and being upstaged by the Commission and national governments, usually covertly but sometimes overtly. Thus, even though the institution has acquired real power in co-decision, conciliation, and budgetary procedures, national electorates are barely aware of this. As seen by many MEPs the 'democratic deficit' is much more apparent than real. The real problem, as they see it, is to mobilise electors to support Parliament's efforts to use its powers and influence in their interest.

The Context for British Journalists and Voters

The pattern of EP coverage is significant. For voters local media coverage frames the Parliament in several ways. Firstly it personalises it – stories stress what the MEP has done for the constituency. Secondly the presentation is often ideological about EU – voters are urged to understand what the Union might do for them, or to them, in the future. Thirdly, the Parliament is presented as an arena for the grand gesture, for example on landmines or civil rights in Turkey. What the coverage does not conceal is that Parliament is costly and, as an institution, lacks both political theatre and the power to topple a government in the Westminster sense. Well-meaning and useful for some initiatives as it is, Parliament is seen as operating 'at the margins'. By contrast British voters think that Westminster still controls defence, foreign policy, interest rates and market regulation – all questionable beliefs. Most ambitious politicians continue to want to be

MPs not MEPs, Cabinet Ministers in London not Commissioners in Brussels. The British constitution, and conventions derived from it, tend to confer on party leaderships, after minimal consultation with followers in and out of Parliament, the power to decide and execute policy in ways not normally possible for governments in many member states.

Journalists reflect these facts. The EU is not a state, as they see it, and its Parliament is not the arena in which an EU 'government' must maintain its support. Hence MEPs are portrayed as less prestigious than MPs and the latter, anyway, as journalists know, have forfeited much prestige of late. If journalists are tempted to question these views, political leaderships in London are very ready to instruct them, usually via their editors. The latter can insist that coverage reflects the view that it is still the case that the Westminster-Whitehall game is the most important British political game. Thus EU is still portrayed as a 'state in waiting' but one which may never emerge fully fledged, and may yet fail to overcome the obstacles inherent in creating single economic, foreign and defence policies.

This is the context of Parliament's 'invisibility' and it has a considerable downside. Parliament is seen as a 'talking shop' and its members find difficulty countering this view with the reality of Parliament's growing influence. MEPs do not appear to be a visible part of party government in the UK and do not play significant roles in party organisations. Conversely invisibility has some useful outcomes. Parliament is still barely seen as a serious threat to the Westminster Parliament and, because it is invisible, it has not become the object of the degree of disdain for politicians that the period 1994–96 has witnessed. This meant that MEPs could get on with their constituency work unimpaired. Voters and groups increasingly used their services and MEPs know which among them has priority. Boundary maintenance – territorial and party – thus had some advantages. Labour voters, for example, when faced with a sitting Conservative MP often write to their Labour MEP with queries on many issues. Law and convention means that most of these have to be forwarded to the MP, unless the MEP sees a European dimension.

The Parliament for some time has struck local chords even though it is not seen as the final embodiment of democratic accountability within the EU. Earlier comparisons with the US Congress are thus not yet relevant since, for the UK, it is the national Parliament which, in theory, deals with life or death questions of foreign and defence policy. Closer integration and subsidiarity, however, would give the parallel greater validity since these functions would be taken over by EU institutions and national parliaments would then deal with most of the second class political questions exactly as US states, now recovering greater autonomy, are doing.

Visibility for the Parliament has to be a part of increased salience for the EU in general so far as the UK is concerned. Importantly, however, greater salience for the Parliament would almost certainly increase that for EU and could increase public trust in its aims and structures in all member countries. At this point it may be worth noting that Parliament, in fact, is acquiring more television coverage in member countries. It was observed earlier that most British MEPs saw television coverage as crucial to securing more press coverage in the UK – to break through what some saw as almost a conspiracy of silence among British newspaper editors. Such views were not peculiarly British and Parliament has taken steps to increase television coverage. In May 1995 Parliament began to use the Commission's rented frequency Europe by Satellite (EbS) for transmitting its key legislative events – debates, press conferences, committee meetings etc. During plenary sessions in Strasbourg debates are now broadcast live on Tuesday, Wednesday and Thursday and, additionally, so are some press conferences.

In December 1996 Parliament's Vice President Anastassoupoulos reported back on the first 18 months of the services provided by the Parliament's Audiovisual Division (Doc PE 245.958/BUR). The general conclusions were encouraging. The expected surge in the election year coverage in 1994 had been exceeded in 1995. On nearly all fronts – number of hours, programmes, live broadcasts, independently produced programmes – the totals were up, sometimes dramatically so. The Report noted that 'the level of audiovisual activity and the scope of television coverage will be closely linked to the nature of Parliament's proceedings themselves and the working conditions enjoyed by the representatives of the press' (Report, p. 3). The Audiovisual Division promised that it would continue to cultivate closer relations with television stations, especially regional television stations, and cooperate with television press agencies.

National variations there were, of course. The surge of interest in 1994 is especially clear in all the larger countries except Italy. The decline thereafter is also clear except in Italy and, interestingly, in the UK. It should be noted, however, that the latter appears in the top four countries in terms of total reports in each of the three years 1993–96. Mr Anastassoupoulos, in his opening remarks, had asked rhetorically:

> Do I need to remind you that the widest possible television coverage of Parliament's activities should remain one of our top priorities and that every

assistance to our Audiovisual Division needed to facilitate this coverage should be accorded (Report, p. 1).

For the Vice President, since 70 per cent of EU citizens relied on television for information on the EU, then television must be the hope of the future for the European Parliament.

British evidence seems to validate some of the Vice President's hope. The Report of the Independent Television Commission confirmed that most voters in the 1 May 1997 election took their information from television coverage. Most voters thought that the coverage was fair though a minority felt it gave anti-EU opinion too much air time (Sancho-Aldridge, 1997). Fifty per cent of the sample were interested in the EU dimension and a third of these claimed that the EU would play a part in their voting intentions. Of course this data does not tell us which way such voters cast their votes. The pre-election poll data clearly suggested that voters favouring the Labour Party were more favourably disposed to EU. The election result and the failure of Labour to convert a large margin of support in the poll data into actual votes – though not seats in Parliament – suggests that any relationship between media, especially television coverage, and pro-EU voting is complex. The activities of the Labour government since 1 May, on EMU and other matters, do not suggest an uncritical pro-EU stance, a fact that media coverage has not failed to highlight. Television coverage of EU, if it were to be considerably increased in member countries, is certainly likely to increase the level of knowledge on EU affairs but that, in itself, does not guarantee increased affection or support for the European Parliament.

Only when such knowledge is fostered and underpinned by national political elites, national political parties and their supporters will it be evaluated and legitimated in ways conducive to further integration. The dilemma is made clear in a recent collection of essays on democratic legitimacy and internationalised governance (Niedermayer and Sinnot, 1995). As Richard Sinnot makes clear in the conclusion:

> The process of transcending the nation state depends on state agents to initiate – or at least to acquiesce in – and implement the necessary measures, and depends on national political actors and processes to persuade national publics to legitimise them (p. 457).

British governments prior to 1 May 1997 were clearly loath to be part of such a legitimation. It remains to be seen how much more willing is the current government.

All of which is evidence of the power of national and Euro elites, via institutional means, to constrain the increasing power and influence of Parliament and, up to a point, to conceal the fact that they are concealing it. Many British MEPs would agree with the point made by Juliet Lodge which was quoted at the outset – namely that not until Parliament is ready, or is driven to, open conflict with the Commission and Council of Ministers will journalists and the public be jolted into new perceptions about the power and roles of the institution. British MEPs may reflect that the history of the Westminster Parliament amply supports this view. The possessors of power, they realise, rarely concede it to others without sometimes acute political conflict.

Epilogue

Perhaps we may leave the last word on the democratic deficit to EU public opinion as measured in Eurobarometer 47. While too much weight must not be placed on snapshot poll data they are, nevertheless, of value when viewed in sequence over time.

On the question of voter awareness of EU in media coverage each election period increased awareness noticeably – 50–66 per cent in 1979, 46–75 per cent in 1984, 45–70 per cent in 1989, and 52 per cent to 63 per cent in 1994–95. Following such election peaks awareness declined rapidly after each of the above elections, though more slowly after 1994. Nevertheless the April–June 1997 EU figure was 54 per cent (down 9 per cent), and the national figures were UK 45 per cent (minus 14 per cent), Ireland 38 per cent (minus 5 per cent) and Belgium 40 per cent (minus 13 per cent).

Asked about the current importance of the European Parliament the EU average figure was 58 per cent claiming that the Parliament was 'important or very important'. The national figures were UK 59 per cent, Belgium 49 per cent and Ireland 67 per cent. On the measure of 'desired importance' of EP, however, all three countries fell below the EU average figure of 46 per cent who wished the Parliament to be 'more important'.

Asked about institutional effectiveness Parliament was seen as marginally the most 'reliable' of EU institutions, 38 per cent compared with the Commission at 36 per cent and the Council of Ministers at 34 per cent. The national figures here were 26 per cent for the UK, 34 per cent for Belgium and 51 per cent for Ireland. On the related question of the

Parliament as 'protector of citizens' interests', the EU figure was 37 per cent with the UK at 43 per cent, Belgium at 29 per cent and Ireland at 67 per cent. A measure of the significance of these figures may be gained appreciating that the EU figure for the 'reliability' of national parliaments and governments was only 40 per cent.

On the question of preferred policy priorities for the Parliament the EU average figures were employment 61 per cent, drugs and crime 39 per cent, environment 36 per cent and cancer/AIDS policies 24 per cent. National figures showed agreement on employment and drugs and crime as top priorities with the other policies competing for third and fourth positions. Belgium alone mentioned consumer protection and only the UK placed human rights in these categories.

Ireland clearly was the most satisfied with EU though marginally least aware of the Union in its media. Belgium ascribed the least current importance to the EP and saw it as the least protective of citizens' rights. By contrast the UK seemed to be the most aware of EU, ascribed high importance and high interest protection to the Parliament.

When we consider support for the EU generally the pattern was quite clear. The EU average was 46 per cent with Ireland being at 80 per cent, Belgium 41 per cent, and the UK 36 per cent. Similar patterns were visible in perceptions of benefit from EU membership – Ireland 88 per cent, Belgium and the UK 36 per cent. Decline in member support for EU membership went from an EU average of 60 per cent in 1990 to 41 per cent in 1997. Both the UK and Belgium paralleled this decline but in Ireland the figure rose from 80 per cent to 88 per cent – undoubtedly a reflection on the Irish Presidency.

Ireland was clearly the most supportive of the three countries on almost every axis – a situation possibly explicable in terms of its 'all gain, no pain' from membership thus far. Whether such strong support will survive the reform of the CAP remains to be seen. Belgium and the UK have reservations both on membership and on outcomes from the Union. More generally, reservations about such membership may be observed in the patterns of social support, or the lack of it, among all members. As EB 47 observed there are 'high correlations between support for the Union and higher educational levels, occupation and the top income quartile' with, additionally, a gender gap of nearly 10 per cent between male and female totals (p. 5). When respondents were questioned about the Parliament as the protector of citizens' interests the responses provided interesting supplementary detail. It observed:

On the political left – right scale we find that both the extreme left and the extreme right feel less well represented than those who define themselves nearer to the centre of the political spectrum. Occupational status shows, as would be expected, that managers feel well represented and the unemployed poorly represented; interestingly however the self employed also feel less well represented than all other active persons (p. 44).

If the EU is not to be seen as a union of the 'comfortable' then more urgent steps must be taken to make its appeal more socially inclusive. The 'comfortable' are the best organised politically and hence gain easy access to the bureaucracy. The self-defined excluded need a platform they can trust. The Parliament has to be that platform and must be seen to be so. Not to ensure that situation is to invite political instability and an almost certain regression in the process of European integration.

References

Anastassopoulos, Georgios (1996), 'On Television Coverage of the Activities of the European Parliament', December, Doc PE 245.958/BUR.
Andersen, Svein S. and Kjell A. Eliassen (1996), 'Traditional Concerns in New Institutional Settings' in ibid. (eds), *The European Union: How Democratic Is It?*, London: Sage.
Butler, Sir Robin (1997), letter to Wayne David MEP, 12 March.
Cohen, Bernard (1963), *The Press and Foreign Policy*, Princeton, NJ: Princeton University Press.
Corbett, Richard, Francis Jacobs and Michael Shackleton (1995), *The European Parliament*, London: Cartermill.
Crawley, John (1996), 'European Integration: Sociological Process or Political Process?', *Innovation. The European Journal of Social Sciences*, 9, 2, June.
Curran, James and Jean Seaton (1988), *Power Without Responsibility. The Press and Broadcasting in Britain*, London: Routledge.
Davidson, David H. and Walter J. Oleszek (1990), *Congress and its Members*, Washington, D.C.: Congressional Quarterly Press.
DeClercq, Willy (1993), *Reflection on Information and Communication Policy of the European Community*, European Commission R.P./1051/93.
Dimmock, Michael A. and Samuel L. Popkin (1997), 'Political Knowledge in Comparative Perspective' in Iyengar, Shanto and Richard Reeves (eds), *Do Media Govern? Politicians, Voters and Reporters in America*, London: Sage.
Duignan, Peter and L.H. Gann (1994), *The USA and the New Europe*, Oxford: Blackwell.
Dyson, Kenneth and Peter Humphreys (1986), *The Politics of the Communication Revolution in Western Europe*, London: Frank Cass.
Earnshaw, David and David Judge (1995), 'From Co-operation to Co-decision: The European Parliament's Path to Legislative Power' in Richardson, Jeremy (ed.), *European Union: Power and Policy-Making*, London: Routledge.
Eurobarometer: EB 45, Spring 1996; EB 46, Autumn 1996: EB 47, Autumn 1997.
Euromedia (1996), 'European Union Press and Television Analysis, February–November 1996', Brussels: Report International for DGX.
European Parliament (1994), *DG III European Elections*, PE 177.792/fin.
EP News (Irish Ed.) (1996), 'Ireland Backs Enhanced Roles for MEPs' p. 1.; 'Citizens First – Your Right to Know and Be Heard', 9–13 December, pp. 1–2.
Fenno, Richard (1978), *Home Style. House Members in Their Districts*, Boston: Little Brown.

George, Stephen (1990), *An Awkward Partner. Britain in the European Community*, Oxford: Oxford University Press.
Greenstein, Fred I. (1980), 'Change and Continuity in the Modern Presidency' in Samuel H. Beer (ed.), *The New American Political System*, Washington, D.C.: American Enterprise Institute.
Harris, Robert (1990), *Good and Faithful Servant*, London: Faber and Faber.
Hill and Knowlton (1996), 'Report on the European Parliament's Communication and Information Policy', London: Hill and Knowlton, January, PE 194.867/BUR.
Iyengar, Shanto and Donald R. Kinder (1987), *News That Matters. Television and American Opinion*, Chicago: Chicago University Press.
Iyengar, Shanto and Richard Reeves (eds) (1997), *Do Media Govern? Politicians, Voters and Reporters in America*, London: Sage.
Liverpool Project (1996), DG X funded, July.
Lodge, Juliet (1996), 'The European Parliament' in Andersen, Svein S. and Kjell A. Eliassen (eds), *The European Union: How Democratic is it?*, London: Sage.
McQuail, Denis (1992), *Media Performance. Mass Communication and the Public Interest*, London: Sage.
Morgan, David (1986), *The Flacks of Washington. Government Information and the Public Agenda*, Westport, CT: Greenwood Press.
Morgan, David (1991), 'Media-Government Relations. The Right to Manage Information versus the right to know', *Parliamentary Affairs*, 44, 4, October, pp. 531–40.
Morgan, David (1995), 'British Media and European Union News. The Brussels News Beat and its Problems', *European Journal of Communication*, 10, 3, September, pp. 321–43.
Morgan, David (1995), 'The British Press Corps in Brussels – the View From the Commission', *British Journalism Review*, 6,4, September, pp. 58–60.
Neidermayer, Oscar and R. Sinnot (eds) (1995), *Public Opinion and Internationalised Governance*, Oxford: Oxford University Press.
Norton, Philip (1995), 'Parliament's Changing Role' in Pyper, Robert and Lynton Robbins (eds), *Governing the UK in the 1990s*, London: St Martin's Press.
Nugent, Neil (1989), *The Government and Politics of the European Community*, London: Macmillan.
Paletz, David L. and Robert M. Entman (1981), *Media. Power. Politics*, New York: Free Press.
Petersen, John (1997), 'The European Union. Pooled Sovereignty, Divided Accountability', *Political Studies*, 45, 3, pp. 559–78.
Pilling, Rod (1994), 'Changing News Values at ITN', MA thesis, Department of Politics, Keele University.
Policy Studies Institute (1987), *Public Image of the European Parliament*, London: Policy Studies Institute.

Sancho-Aldridge, Jane (1997), 'Election, '97 Viewers' Responses to the Television Coverage', London: Independent Television Commission.

Santer, Jacques (1997), 'I cannot accept an à la carte Europe', *The European*, 13–19 February, pp. 10–11.

Schlesinger, Philip (1996), 'From Cultural Protection to Political Culture. Media Policy and the European Union', paper presented at the *Euroconference on Collective Identity and Symbolic Representation*, Paris, July.

Skocpol, Theda (1985), 'Bringing the State Back In' in Evans, Peter B., D. Rueschemeyer, and T. Skocpol (eds), *Bringing the State Back In*, Cambridge: Cambridge University Press.

Smart, Victor (1996), 'Britain the Uncertain Partner', *The European*, 5–11 December, p. 10.

Tartwyk-Novey, Louise B. Van (1995), *The European House of Cards. Towards a United States of Europe*, Basingstoke: Macmillan.

The European, 5–11 December, 1996; 23–29 January, 1997; 13–19 February, 1997; 26 June–2 July, 1997.

The Times (1997), 'Labour Rebels Risk Expulsion', 22 October, p. 10.